Dave's story and choices narrated in *Good Work* of Jesus would do well to ponder. In an age where reputation, his simple message of us seeking first _ goodness and living that out in our workplaces will do a whole lot to make our faith relevant and the "gospel" actually good news.

ANDREW CAMPBELL
Owner of Beaverhill Woodcrafters, Plain, WA

A machinist with a doctoral degree—you don't meet one of those every day. Nor will you often find a book that so effectively demonstrates the hand-in-glove relationship between faith and everyday work. In *Good Work*, David Hataj has given us a wide-open window into his years of experience in the "real world." Hataj meshes making gears with serving God—not merely in theory but in actual practice. His story traces the painful path he traveled to make that faith-work connection. *Good Work* will expand your outlook on family health, meaningful work, integrity in business, mentoring, and bridging the generation gap.

LARRY PEABODY
Professor, Theology of Work, Bakke Graduate University; author, *Job-Shadowing Daniel: Walking the Talk at Work*

You will want to pass Dave Hataj's *Good Work* on to every small business owner, especially those in the trades. Kingdom impact is possible in blue collar business. Dave's secret sauce to integrating faith in the workplace is "DO WHAT YOU SAY YOU ARE GOING TO DO!!!" I could not put the book down, reading it all in two sittings. I resonated with what Dave has to say—my father was a machinist and also a pastor, both in church and in the machine shop. It felt like Dave was in the room with me all the time reminding me that God is infinitely more concerned with who we become than with what we accomplish.

WILLY KOTIUGA
Chair, Bakke Graduate University Board of Regents

As a business professional, church elder, men's ministry leader, and personal friend, I can testify that Dave is a man that truly lives the words of Jesus, "You are the salt of the earth" and "the light of the world . . . that they may see your good deeds and glorify your Father in heaven" (Matt 5:13–16). Dave and his life story in *Good Work* is the application our men's ministry has spent years trying to teach men; our workplace and business is the mission field and not a secular job. *Good Work* is now our handbook.

GREG KING
Chief Experience Officer, ExponentHR
Elder, Trinity Bible Church, Richardson, TX

Get ready, *Good Work* is going to challenge who you are not only in the workplace, but in your community, family and in all your relationships. *Good Work* is good stuff . . . God stuff.

SCOTT HAMMOND
Elder at Calvary Memorial Church, Oak Park, IL and Business Development in Technology of a large corporation

Inspiring to learn how doing the right thing ethically and morally can equal success. A great story of how life's challenges were overcome by faith and ethical business. As a twenty-year employee, I was blown away to learn the goal of the business was not money.

BRENT SCHROEDER
Team leader, lead mentor, and customer service at Edgerton Gear

Considering conversations over twenty-five years in board rooms with my large investment banking corporate clients, I am taken by how powerful are the words in this book from the owner/operator of a small machine shop to drive excellence in any business. The themes of basing business decisions on "inner goodness" and integrity can be a powerful influence to leaders of businesses of any size.

MICHAEL JONES
Managing Director, Investment Banking

Dave Hataj loves Jesus and this book is a testament to a life lived in pursuit of Him! It is the story of Jesus' faithfulness, gentleness, and heart cry for each and every person made in His image, including those of us who find ourselves in a blue collar world. This is a unique and essential contribution to the "faith and work" conversation that, if ignored, is done so at the peril of the Christian church around the globe. Finally, and somewhat less obviously, it is proof that behind every married man, there is a strong and loving woman. Without Tracy, the pages of this book would lie empty.

JOSIAH WARREN
Carpenter

An unapologetically Christian guide to fulfilling our life's purpose in the workplace. The book is written with a degree of honesty and practicality that would benefit anyone looking for direction in life, especially at the workplace. Business is so often associated with greed and money, however, it can also be a source of love and purpose. *Dave concisely lays out how to align our values with a greater purpose than money*, and I would recommend this book to Christians and non-Christians alike who wish to do the same.

COLE SAMUELSON
Temporary Worker at Edgerton Gear

If wisdom is the insight distilled from a lifetime of experience by a thoughtful and faithful practitioner, then Dave Hataj's book, *Good Work*, is a veritable pearl necklace of practical wisdom.

RANDY FRANZ
Professor of management at Seattle Pacific University

Dave Hataj does a wonderful job explaining how God's righteousness extends to every aspect of our lives, including the business world. This is a must read for every business owner.

KEITH CAMPBELL
Chairman of Mannington Mills, Inc.

GOOD WORK

HOW BLUE COLLAR BUSINESS CAN CHANGE LIVES, COMMUNITIES, AND THE WORLD

DAVE HATAJ

MOODY PUBLISHERS

CHICAGO

All Scripture quotations, unless otherwise indicated, are taken from the Holy Bible, New International Version®, NIV®. Copyright © 1973, 1978, 1984, 2011 by Biblica, Inc.™ Used by permission of Zondervan. All rights reserved worldwide. www.zondervan.com. The "NIV" and "New International Version" are trademarks registered in the United States Patent and Trademark Office by Biblica, a Division of Tyndale House Ministries.

Scripture quotations marked MSG are taken from *The Message,* copyright © 1993, 2002, 2018 by Eugene H. Peterson. Used by permission of NavPress. All rights reserved. Represented by Tyndale House Publishers, a Division of Tyndale House Ministries.

Scripture quotations marked KJV are taken from the King James Version.

Names and details of some stories have been changed to protect the privacy of individuals.

Published in association with the literary agent of Mark Sweeney & Associates, Bonita Springs, Florida.

Edited by Kevin P. Emmert
Interior design: Ragont Design
Cover design: Erik M. Peterson
Cover photo of gear in workshop copyright © 2016 by Bisual Studio / Stocksy (1047452). All rights reserved.

Library of Congress Cataloging-in-Publication Data

Names: Hataj, Dave, author.
Title: Good work : how blue collar business can change lives, communities, and the world / Dave Hataj.
Description: Chicago : Moody Publishers, 2020. | Includes bibliographical references. | Summary: "What can blue-collar business teach us all about work and faith? The faith and work conversation is alive and well, but most resources focus on white-collar jobs and neglect the majority of the workforce. When pastor Dave Hataj realized he needed to go home and take over the family gear shop, he didn't really expect it to become a spiritually transformative season of his life. Yet as he began to think about what it meant to be a Christian in business, he discovered just how much our work matters to God and how blue-collar business really can change people, communities, and even the world. Drawing on the stories of his business, Edgerton Gears, Dave teaches you how to cultivate true inner goodness (righteousness), meaning, and mission at work-no matter what you do. Your workplace can and should be a place of significance. Find out how today"-- Provided by publisher.
Identifiers: LCCN 2019046400 (print) | LCCN 2019046401 (ebook) | ISBN 9780802419576 (paperback) | ISBN 9780802496485 (ebook)
Subjects: LCSH: Work--Religious aspects--Christianity. | Business--Religious aspects--Christianity. | Blue collar workers--Religious life.
Classification: LCC BT738.5 .H375 2020 (print) | LCC BT738.5 (ebook) | DDC 248.8/8--dc23
LC record available at https://lccn.loc.gov/2019046400
LC ebook record available at https://lccn.loc.gov/2019046401

Originally delivered by fleets of horse-drawn wagons, the affordable paperbacks from D. L. Moody's publishing house resourced the church and served everyday people. Now, after more than 125 years of publishing and ministry, Moody Publishers' mission remains the same—even if our delivery systems have changed a bit. For more information on other books (and resources) created from a biblical perspective, go to: www.moodypublishers.com or write to:

Moody Publishers
820 N. LaSalle Boulevard
Chicago, IL 60610

1 3 5 7 9 10 8 6 4 2

Printed in the United States of America

Dedicated to Tracy, my bride of thirty years and counting, whose steadfast support and encouragement is more than any man deserves, and who has endured more than any wife should.

Contents

Foreword

David Hataj is more than a former student. He is a soul friend and an exemplar.

If, as is so often said, the most personal is the most universal, then his story of the integration of faith and work is something that will touch and transform your story, as it has mine. Growing up with gear grease on his hands, the last thing he wanted to do was take over his father's precision gear manufacturing business. That is precisely what he was led to do, and he did it with gusto. Faith gusto. Love gusto. Hope gusto.

Before doing it, he had set up a ministry development project with me at Regent College, a project to bring some health to his family and his family's business by the application of Christian leadership and management principles. That six-month project became a three-year, grueling, God-soaked experience for him and, to some extent, for me.

I would be reading his reports on a plane visiting him in Edgerton, Wisconsin, with tears streaming down my face. But that project is not simply what you are about to read. The book he has crafted is truth squeezed through personality and personal work experience. And it is not just three years of heart revelation but a couple of decades. What you will explore, as you read this book—no, better, as you live through it—is something that will show how one person (and by implication you and me, too) can integrate faith and work, making Monday to Friday (or Saturday) a full-time ministry experience.

Nicely and deliciously, David ministers not only to his employees and clients but, as you will see, now quite widely in the school system to help young people integrate head, hands, and heart in a holistic work experience that is practical and neighbor-loving.

And why?

One of the most serious processes to happen in the church over the centuries—briefly nullified in the Protestant Reformation and with some Catholic renewal movements—is *dualism*. That's the idea that certain works, such as being a pastor or missionary, are sacred, while reengineering gears on a sophisticated gear-hobbing machine, and dealing with recalcitrant customers, are secular.

That has driven a whole generation of faith-people into professional ministry, if they really want to serve God "full-time." One of those persons originally influenced by this practical heresy was David Hataj. But through a process of study and immersion in faith-based business ventures, and finally by taking the plunge into the family business, David became convinced that he was "doing the Lord's work."

You can, too. Perhaps you will, after reading this book. After all, Jesus spent a couple of decades hammering, sawing, and figuring out solutions to building problems, while the world was going to hell in a handbasket. But at His baptism, God the Father said "with him I am well pleased."

Integrating faith and work is not just "using" faith to gain effectiveness in the workplace. Perhaps it will, since a common complaint I hear from Christian executives is that their employees don't "get into" their work, so busy and motivated are they with church activities and Bible studies.

Will workplace spirituality increase the excellence with which we work? Possibly, though if we are workaholics, we might become less obsessed with perfection with a true integration of faith and work.

Will workplace spirituality enable us to please God irrespective of whether we have a high-profile job that obviously benefits people directly, or a behind-the-scenes service job? Yes, absolutely.

Will workplace spirituality affect our attitude toward superiors and subordinates? Yes, definitely, since we will know that ultimately we are working for Christ, as Paul affirms: "It is the Lord Christ you are serving" (Col. 3:24).

Will workplace spirituality enable us to see through situations, problems, and conflicts, and grow through them? Without a doubt.

Will workplace spirituality give us more satisfaction in our daily work? Possibly, but our satisfaction will not mainly be in the work itself but in God, in the context of our work.

Will workplace spirituality empower us to become better witnesses for God and faith? Probably, but not because we have learned a new technique. Rather, we will have more depth and sensitivity to the Spirit's leading as we experience God in the workplace. So, to use Jesus' metaphor, the key thing is to have salt in ourselves (Mark 9:50).

Yes! Read this book.

Read the person.

Read the experience.

Read the hungering and searching God within the experience.

And get some salt in yourself.

R. Paul Stevens
Chairman, Institute for Marketplace Transformation
Professor Emeritus
Marketplace Theology
Regent College, Vancouver, BC

Introduction

Gears and God's Kingdom

I often think the modern workplace is like a set of worn out, misaligned gears. When gears are damaged and not meshing properly, bad things happen. The entire machine suffers, the other components can't function as they were meant to, and the whole system breaks down.

You could be in any profession; wherever you work, you undoubtedly have experienced a measure of frustration, brokenness, and chaos. Over and over, you've told yourself, "This job shouldn't be so hard!" Things go wrong, people don't follow through, bosses make unreasonable demands, coworkers can be moody and even impossible to work with.

We sense that somewhere down in the bowels of the machine of our workplace, something is deeply broken. Yet we often struggle along, earning a paycheck because we need to, longing for the weekend to escape the trials, tribulations, and the soul-sucking hours we spend "at work."

But is this just the way things are? Is work indeed a curse or was it meant to be a gift?

My name is Dave Hataj (HAY-tag). I'm a second-generation owner of a family business in Wisconsin. I didn't choose the business; I wished my parents had started a ski resort or a hunting lodge.

But gear making is what my dad knew. It was his way of supporting our family. Growing up, it became my only option as well. I've struggled with the shop being dirty, tedious, demeaning, and prison-like. I couldn't wait to make my escape, yet now, all these years later, I find myself stunned to admit that I love it. For over the last four decades, I've come to conclude the modern workplace, as broken as it is, can be a place of deep significance and life-affirming community.

Edgerton Gear, Incorporated is our corner of that modern workplace. Since 1962, it's been manufacturing precision custom gears for all sorts of equipment. I'm often asked what I do for a living. The conversation then goes something like this:

"I make gears."

"Oh, like sports gear or camping gear?"

"No, we make gears—those things that make different kinds of machines run."

"Um, what kind of machines? Like bicycles? Do you make that thing with those pointy things the chain goes around?

"Well, yes—but that's a sprocket. We do make quite a few sprockets. And those pointy things are called *teeth*. But mostly we make gears. They may be as small as an inch in diameter, or as big as five feet. You may not realize it, but gears are everywhere, and modern civilization would not exist without them."

The conversation usually ends there, as most people can't

imagine how integral gears, sprockets, and pulleys are to keeping our modern world humming. Gears are usually hidden under safety covers or are deep within the machines. Yet they are powerful, and even mysterious to most people.

My parents founded the business on three founding principles: quality, value, and service—terms that are easily thrown around these days, but are too often more slogans than reality.

What do these values look like in the day-to-day operations? Since taking the helm of our family business in 1992, I've wrestled with keeping our company grounded in these values, keeping it profitable, keeping up with the technological changes, and having our business be a place that emphasizes a deeper purpose and quality relationships. It hasn't been a smooth ride, but it's been worthwhile.

I never imagined myself writing a book. In fact, when my wife and others would tell me I needed to share my beliefs and thoughts about work with the world, I'd dismiss them by saying there are already too many books out there. However, a severe illness rocked my world and put me on the couch for a couple of years, forcing me to rest. As my energy slowly returned, I, faced with the realization of my mortality, felt the urge to put down on paper what our guiding principles are for our small company. I also realized that most books about business are written from a white collar, executive level, or by business consultants or professors. I don't recall ever reading a book from a blue-collar perspective.

I live in a blue-collar world, and I wouldn't want it any other way. Although our company looks quite a bit different from its early years, when there were no computers or internet, I still refer to it as "the shop," as in "a machine shop." I still change into a machinist's uniform when I get to work.

My father was often brutally honest. When he'd again embarrass us in various public and private settings by laying out the truth with little or no tact, he'd comically say, "I calls 'em like I sees 'em." In our shop, honesty is pretty important, even controversial. It's not my intention to offend anyone, but I do have to be honest with my convictions. You may not agree with me on everything, but that's not a requirement for you to enjoy the book and get something out of it. I value openness and honesty from others, and so I wanted to give that to you at the beginning.

Without apology, you'll notice I definitely have a religious bent to my writing. In today's conflicted and pluralistic culture, tolerance for another's views and beliefs is often held as the highest virtue, except when it comes to having Judeo-Christian beliefs. Christians and Jews often feel the need to apologize for their beliefs, which I refuse to do.

Granted, every belief system has members who are extreme and therefore intolerant and judgmental of others. Everyone has a belief system or worldview of some kind.

I grew up in a home where I was caught between one parent who was a devout Christian and the other who was an angry atheist. So as an adult, I ventured on a journey to discover not only what belief system had the most validity, but also what made practical sense in my day-to-day life. As objectively as I could, I examined every belief system I came into contact with, attempting to screen out the more extreme elements of each.

Perhaps not surprisingly, in the end, I became a serious and devout follower of Jesus of Nazareth. I hesitate to identify myself as "Christian" at times because of all the cultural connotations and baggage associated with the term. This lesson was learned during numerous trips to Honduras, working with the rural poor. If anyone identified themselves as Catholic, Protestant, or Muslim, they were immediately labeled with the associated traits and prejudices. I find it more "neutral" simply to identify myself as a follower of Jesus.

I don't proselytize my faith at work or in other areas of life, but I'm deeply spiritual. I take the teachings of Jesus seriously in how I conduct business. I don't require my staff to share my spiritual beliefs, but I do require us all to have shared values and be unified in our sense of mission.

As with any business, if you don't like what a company stands for, you don't have to work there or purchase its products. We're not a cult or prison, but we're very passionate about making the best gears possible to meet our customers' needs. My belief system has taught me that we're all meant to do something worthwhile during our time on this planet. For a small group of us, making gears is worthwhile, as it offers our hands a creative outlet for our hearts and heads. We know we're making the world a better place through our work, and there are few things more satisfying in life.

I believe this is one of the greatest heart cries of everyone who has ever lived. I also believe business is one of the primary vehicles for us as humans to do something worthwhile.

In the following pages, I propose that seeking God's kingdom and His righteousness—something we'll explore later—should or could be the determining factor in not only how one conducts business, but how we do life in general. I'll attempt to convey what I believe is God's vision for our world and how business is to be done, drawing on the parables and teachings of Jesus.

I believe Jesus had more to say about how to run a business than we have yet realized. Just as every generation must rediscover the relevancy of faith, we, in our ongoing struggle against greed and deceit, need God's Word to speak into our day-to-day transactions and to give us a vision for the true riches of His kingdom as that relates to business. It's my conviction, born out of more than four decades connected to the family shop, that the workplace—especially small businesses—provide infinite opportunities for the practical application of faith, hope, and love.

This book is my attempt to apply some moral, ethical, and spiritual foundations to the workplace in order to make it more fulfilling and having more impact than the plain process of making money. If you work for or own a small- or medium-sized business, I'm confident you'll be able to relate to my experiences and stories.

If you're trying to figure out how faith and work are connected, I hope you'll be inspired to join the ranks of those of us who recognize we're uniquely positioned to have a profound influence for the good in people's lives, and to run your business accordingly.

If you belong to a large corporation, it's my hope you'll be able to glean something useful, while also gaining an appreciation for us little guys who are part of your supply chain.

Whatever your role in the workplace, you have a sphere of influence that has more of an impact on those around you than you may realize.

Called to Do Business

Two percent! It was only 2 percent. Was I willing to risk losing our biggest customer over a measly 2 percent reduction in our pricing?

I'd driven three hours to visit this customer, who comprised approximately 7 percent of our annual sales. I'd prayed for wisdom, since I knew I'd be on the hot seat. The customer had recently been bought out by a larger corporation, whose culture it was to hammer vendors by insisting they lower their prices if they were to continue doing business with them.

It didn't matter that health insurance for our staff was rising 10 to 15 percent annually, that raw material prices were up, along with wages, utilities, and taxes. The new corporation's strategy was to send in a hatchet man from corporate headquarters and, along with the purchasing agents, bring in the vendors one at a time to bully them into submission. It was now my turn.

A gear is a simple machine based on the principle of rotation. It's a variation of the wheel, that simplest of machines. But where a wheel might work alone, a gear is a wheel that moves other wheels, using its cogs or teeth.

Once a series of gears mesh, tooth to tooth, a more complex machine operates, and greater tasks can be done. I've watched, helped build, and sold many thousands of gears over the decades. Round and round they go, wheels within wheels, much like the culture that has grown over the years around our workplace, where the gears are made. Here, people mesh with people. One person's movements and work help another's.

Like teeth engaged with the next gear, we gently assist others along their paths, and keep them from slipping. A kind of dance if you will. And when the human machinery works well, we do greater, more complex work.

If you look up *gear* in the dictionary, you'll see that, when used as a verb, this word means "to fit exactly"; "to be in gear." We motivate someone by saying, "Get it in gear." If you wear your team *gear*, you fit in.

But as we all know, not every job seems a perfect fit. Sometimes the gears of work seem to grind and squeal, nothing is more unpleasant. There's slippage. When gears are damaged, out of alignment with others, or not maintained properly, the results are destructive. They strain other components, breaking down the whole system. It's the same way when we're not a good fit in our job setting.

What is it that makes work *work* for us? How can we bring the pleasing precision to the workplace that we can establish with iron and steel? What has led me to contend the workplace can be a place with a measure of joy, significance, and community?

I didn't choose to be born into a family business; none of us do. It just happens. Before I was in kindergarten, my older sisters and I were down at the shop after dinner, putting set screws into sprockets. We were cheap labor, but that's what Dad needed us to do.

By age seven, I was cleaning out chip barrels, sweeping floors, and wiping down the lathes, mills, and gear hobbers. I was expected to work after school, during summers, and whenever I had a day off from school. By age twenty-one, I was a journeyman machinist and I'd had enough. I ran away to California, swearing I'd never be back. So how in the world was I sitting in this conference room with this "hatchet man," wondering if I should risk calling his bluff?

The ancient rabbis said that a father was obligated to teach his son a trade: "He who does not teach his son a trade teaches him to steal."[1]

My father taught me to be a machinist, not a pastor. But like many young, zealous believers, when God got hold of me at age nineteen, I thought He was calling me to "full-time" ministry, which everyone seemed to define as either being a pastor or a missionary.

I soon found myself on the fast track for a career as a pastor. I did youth ministry, became a donor-supported staff of a parachurch ministry, and eventually found myself on the pastoral staff of a megachurch in Southern California. I even ended up at Regent College, a theological graduate school in Vancouver, BC.

However, during that time, my wife and I believed God was "calling" us back to the one place I swore I'd never return, back to the family business as a gear maker. The business had taken its toll on my father, and he was desperate to retire. He tried selling the company to the employees, but with so little unity among them, they couldn't come up with a fair offer.

His next option was to find an outside buyer. But the shop was his baby, and it would break his heart to see someone overhaul it and possibly cause his staff to lose their jobs. As the only son, I felt a sense of obligation to honor my parents and help transition the business to new ownership so my parents could enjoy their later years. I'd worked at it since age five—I'm sure my dad violated all sorts of child labor laws.

I remember running a power hacksaw when I was about seven. It was bigger than I was. I drove a lift truck by twelve and became pretty proficient on a lathe by fifteen. Shop classes in high school were a breeze, as I probably knew as much or more about machining than our shop teacher—though he did teach me a lot about welding, drafting, and shop math.

By age twenty-one, I could run any machine in the shop; I was running entire departments. But for a variety of reasons, after I left for California shortly before my twenty-second birthday, I knew I'd never be back. I thought I was destined for more than just working in a machine shop, making gears. Supposedly, I had a special calling to do "divine" service to God by being a clergyman.

Then, during my second year of theological school, when I was married with a newborn son, it seemed clear we were to go back to what I considered the darkest and most depressing place on earth.

Could this be true? It was oily and grimy blue-collar work. Pornography and beer were part of the work culture. In fact, there was so much beer that my father even put a quarter-barrel keg in the lunch room refrigerator for the employees. Surely God wasn't calling me back to such a depraved place. What could this possibly have to do with being in "ministry"?

That was more than twenty-five years ago, and guess what? I'm still here! My wife and I originally thought we would come back, help reorganize the company, and after a few years, God would reveal His real plan for our lives; we would be called to go somewhere in the world to do real ministry. Never in my wildest dreams (or nightmares) could I imagine I would eventually be convinced that this little gear shop was exactly where God wanted me for the long haul.

Not only that, I came to believe there was nowhere else in the world I could do such effective "ministry" than in and through this small business.

What changed? Maybe it was just a matter of perspective. Unfortunately, the world's religions don't seem to do an adequate job of affirming most of us in our work worlds. The Christian subculture is especially guilty of conveying the idea that a calling is only for those who work in churches or are missionaries—as in "being called to the ministry."

This is not only wrong, but it's just plain stupid! God uses and orchestrates our life experiences for His purposes.

For many years, I had a hard time believing this. As a young, zealous believer at the age of twenty-one, I desperately wanted to serve God in a significant way. But I was "just" a journeyman machinist. Being a gear maker for God didn't seem significant, adventuresome, or sexy. What could God possibly do with a machinist?

I remember going to two Urbana mission conferences in my twenties, trying to discern God's call for my life as I believed being a missionary was the ultimate act of discipleship—in other words, living my life for God. This conference is held every three years for college students to help them figure out what God may want to do with their lives. I was probably the only machinist out of the nearly 17,000 students, as I wandered up and down the aisles packed with booths of seemingly every mission agency in existence.

I kept asking if this agency or that one could use a machinist. In both conferences, I didn't receive even a maybe! If I couldn't be a pastor, teacher, doctor, social worker, or airplane pilot for the mission field (which to me meant some far away, exotic place), then no one wanted me.

> **Our work is where God calls us to *minister*, to serve.**

The word *ministry* in its simplest form means to serve. We're all called to serve, to be ministers, no matter what our job or profession is. But somewhere along the way, the word got hijacked to refer only to what religious professionals do. One of the unintended consequences of this is that too many of us have come to leave "ministry" to the professionals. We fail to realize how critical our role is in bringing the world in line with how God intended it to be.

As a result, we lose our sense of purpose and fail to embrace our profound influence in cultivating meaningful relationships. We fail to recognize how influential our businesses can be in our communities. Many of us intuitively know that our role in business is important, but the lack of recognition, affirmation, and encouragement we receive from the religious professionals often causes us to doubt and even question whether our work even matters to God.

Thus, we often get involved in some form of volunteer work in a church or a nonprofit organization, thinking there we'll discover and fulfill a sense of calling to ministry. In the meantime, ironically, the one place we spend the majority of our lives is the one place we're actually making the most impact for God's kingdom— in our places at work.

We're fulfilling God's call for our lives and we may not even realize it.

In his book *Why Business Matters to God (And What Still Needs to Be Fixed)*, Jeff Van Duzer addresses the role of business in the grand scheme of God's intent for us to fill the world and make it fruitful.

> There are two legitimate, first order, intrinsic purposes of business: as stewards of God's creation, business leaders should manage their businesses (1) to provide the community with goods and services that will enable it to flourish, and (2) to provide opportunities for meaningful work that will allow employees to express their God-given creativity.[2]

Considering Van Duzer's first purpose of business—providing goods and services for our communities and the world to survive and thrive—the mere fact that you're reading this means your life has probably been touched by the gears we make at Edgerton Gear. Almost every aluminum can, paper cup, tissue, piece of paper, book, and numerous items you use daily have been produced by the assistance of our gears. You're able to enjoy the conveniences of modern life, and probably to do your own work, because machinists and manufacturers build stuff.

Consider Van Duzer's second purpose for business: providing meaningful employment. We supply employment for three dozen or so hardworking, skilled tradespeople who have families, dreams, and unique talents. Edgerton Gear also offers, as our employees often say, a safe place, an environment that is stable, predictable, and open to them expressing their God-given creativity and talents to contribute to the good of the world.

Furthermore, God continues to use this little machine shop to breathe life and hope into numerous young people. We created a curriculum called Craftsman with Character for high school students. These high school students are introduced to the trades and manufacturing as not only a viable career path, but also as an avenue for discovering their uniqueness and place in the world.

Much of the curriculum is based on job shadowing, as the students follow experienced and sometimes crusty machinists, who end up opening their hearts to these kids. And that's exactly what some of these kids need, as they may well be lost and dejected; we often find they don't fit into the current educational model followed by our public schools.

Since 2012, we've had dozens of boys and girls come through our class, held here at Edgerton Gear. Other businesses and school districts have also embraced our curriculum. I've had numerous opportunities to speak with educators, helping to direct the needed change in our local schools. Just recently, I had the privilege of hosting 130 elementary school teachers in our shop, sharing the "good news" of helping young people find their place in the world.

So can business be a "calling"?

I can honestly say my career in business has been more instrumental and fulfilling than it could ever have been if I'd been working in a church building as a pastor. The work world needs pastors too, of course. Yet I can think of no better place to fulfill my calling than in this family business.

Although I originally thought God was calling us back here for not more than five years, it took ten years before what I call Kingdom Values began to take root. Creating a culture rooted in compassion, respect, trust, humility, service, gratitude, and a commitment to excellence is akin to sowing seeds and growing a garden.

The effort, sacrifice, and commitment to cultivate the soil, nurture new growth, and be diligent in dealing with weeds and harmful pests has worn me out over the years. But I'm constantly reminded that this machine shop, which makes gears for equipment all over the world, is God's shop and part of His kingdom. I'm just the caretaker—the steward.

WHAT'S YOUR CALLING?

So what's your calling? Or another way we might ask the question is: What is your life purpose?

What motivates you to get up and go to work every day? Is it to make money? To be your own boss some day? To provide a secure future for you and your family? Are you an entrepreneur who has a burning desire to bring a new product or service to the marketplace? Are you taking over a family business and wanting to keep it going?

Maybe it's all the reasons above. Or maybe you've never really thought about it as anything more than just a job. Whatever your situation or mindset is, let me make one thing perfectly clear: no matter if you're a business owner, a new employee, or in any position in a company, you're in a deeply profound position of influence, whether you want to be or not. What is your sphere of influence where you work?

You're daily making decisions that affect people's lives in numerous ways. Your job is every bit as important as being a pastor in a formal, religious setting such as church. I'll go even further to say you're probably even more influential than most pastors, because you get to spend forty, fifty, or even sixty hours per week with these folks, compared to just a few hours a week that the religious professionals spend with their constituents.

Not only that, you contribute to the financial livelihood, medical care, and to a large extent, the emotional and spiritual health of those around you. You have the power to create an environment that builds them up as God's beloved creations. Or you can tear people down, using and abusing them as mere objects or tools to make you money.

What's your sphere of influence?

Everyone plays a role in creating a life-affirming culture in the workplace. You help set the tone of how much (or little) your coworkers are valued and appreciated. You're also able to either allow them to express their unique gifts and talents—or not. You have a unique role to play in developing and growing the morals and ethics in your workplace. It's in the culture you help create that allows them to grow in their capacity to communicate, and to trust and love others.

You also play a role in reining in the dark sides of others, since being in relationship means calling out and confronting selfishness, bitterness, laziness, jealousies, and prejudices, as these can't be tolerated if you're striving to have your organization exhibit true inner goodness.

Either you embrace this role and recognize it as one of your primary responsibilities in making your workplace better, or you ignore it and eventually wonder why your company is struggling. Ultimately, we all contribute to making our workplaces better or worse. Which side are you on?

Now, if you've been in the workplace for a while, please don't think that I'm trying to put a guilt trip on you, that you're not living up to some super-spiritual sense of calling. On the contrary, it's my hope that you'll be affirmed not only to realize how awesome you are for having the courage and compassion to go to work every day and provide goods, services, and jobs—but that you'll also be inspired to live on a new level of faith, as you recognize how pivotal a role you play in the kingdom of God.

WHY "THE KINGDOM OF GOD"?

By this point, you probably noticed I've used the phrase "the kingdom of God" several times, and you might be wondering why I think it's important.

In my quest to make sense of what I'm doing in a gear shop that smells of cutting oil, steel, and cast-iron dust, I've come to realize that much of what we have come to believe or think about Christianity has much less to do with going to church than it does with the kingdom of God. The words are pretty impressive, especially if you think of James Earl Jones or someone else with a deep baritone voice booming it out. Simply "going to church" doesn't sound nearly as compelling as THE KINGDOM OF GOD, does it?

I may not be thrilled about sitting in a pew, but the possibility of being part of God's kingdom gets my attention.

At age nineteen, I hadn't had much experience in going to church or having a religious education. My mother took me to Sunday school when I was a small child, so I knew some of the major Bible stories, but I was still pretty much a blank slate. In my quest to make sense of the world, I started reading the Bible on my own, which I suppose can be dangerous.

As I read the four gospels (Matthew, Mark, Luke, and John) and took in four different accounts of the life of Jesus, I was impressed by how similar they were and yet different. I later came to understand that it was like four different eyewitnesses giving their story of how they saw and understood a particular time in history. I noticed right away that there wasn't nearly as much talk about "being saved" or church attendance as there was about God's "kingdom."

Jesus repeatedly says things like, "The kingdom of God has come near" and "the kingdom of God is like . . ."

As the scholar and theologian R. Paul Stevens states,

It's not an overstatement to say that the Kingdom of God was the master thought of Jesus. It's used over a hundred times in the Gospels in comparison to only three references to the church. . . .

The Kingdom is not a realm, a territory, but the rule of God as King.[3]

I tend to think Jesus' words about the new "kingdom" resonated on a much deeper level with His listeners than it does with us today. But that doesn't mean His words don't have huge ramifications for those of us in business or in positions of affluence and influence. In fact, I propose that seeking God's kingdom and His righteousness should or could be the determining factor in how we conduct business. But again, if you're wondering what exactly Jesus is talking about, you're not alone. I've been trying to figure this out for the past twenty-six years! I don't claim to have a lot of answers, but I can say with a high degree of confidence that the more I grasp what Jesus was talking about, the greater impact I see our shop making in our community and, ultimately, the world.

THE KINGDOM IN THE WAREHOUSE

Now, many are familiar with Jesus' famous admonition in Matthew 6:33 to seek first God's kingdom and His righteousness. Many of us heard it in church when we were in Sunday school and even sang songs about it. But it's not just a sweet children's song. It's radical and disruptive. These were powerful words back then, and I propose they're still powerful words for us if we understand what they really mean.

Perhaps we've lost how radical this kingdom talk really is. Jesus wasn't referring to being holier-than-thou or religious. There was too much of that already, and it was arguably one of the big problems.

In fact, Jesus hated religion when it got in the way of authentic goodness and how people truly connected with God. Being in God's kingdom wasn't just for Sunday. It should impact every part of our lives, including business. In fact, I argue this especially applies to business, as many of us spend the majority of our lives at work, and this is where the vast majority of our world's corruption takes place.

So what did Jesus mean? For the answer to that question, we

need to step back in time and imagine ourselves in first-century Galilee and Judea, where Jesus lived.

Similar to today, it was a cultural, political, and religious hotbed. Because it was part of the Roman Empire, it was under military rule, with an occupying military force of Romans. Steeped in religious tradition, there were strict religious rules and temple rituals that were to be followed if you were Jewish.

The Romans were concerned about civil unrest and radical uprisings from the poor and marginalized. If you were a Jewish man, at least you had some degree of social respectability, but you were still subjected to Roman laws and oppression. If you were a woman or child, you weren't as fortunate, because your social standing wasn't much higher than that of dogs or cattle.

Human trafficking was common, and the ruling class rigged the system so they could keep their positions of wealth and power. There was no social welfare or easy access to medical care. Begging and prostitution were a means of survival. Being an average citizen was a daily challenge since you never knew who would oppress you next—soldiers, politicians, religious leaders, landowners, or anyone who had a monopoly on power and wealth.

With all the competing forces, it was a dog-eat-dog world. In the midst of all this, Jesus came on the scene announcing a new kingdom and the reign of God.

Naturally, if you occupied a position of power and influence, such talk was considered a threat. Immediately, Jesus was targeted to be silenced and killed if necessary. And yet the masses were drawn to Him. Something about His message and teaching inspired hope, and maybe even provided an answer to being used and abused by a multitude of oppressors.

In this context, imagine this homeless carpenter standing

before the weary masses on a hillside outside of town, who came to hear a possible fresh word from God.

WORDS FOR SEEKERS

"Therefore, I tell you, do not worry about your life, what you will eat or drink; or about your body, what you will wear. Is not life more than food, and the body more than clothes? Look at the birds of the air; they do not sow or reap or store away in barns, and yet your heavenly Father feeds them. Are you not much more valuable than they? Can any one of you by worrying add a single hour to your life?" (Matt. 6:25–27)

Jesus went on to ask why anyone should worry about clothing, when the flowers are clothed beautifully by God while doing no work at all. What's the point of worrying in a world where God cares so wonderfully for birds and flowers? Godless types spend their time chasing their own anxiety, but instead, Jesus says, we should "seek first his kingdom and his righteousness, and all these things will be given to you as well" (v. 33).

I think an argument can be made that the majority of Jesus' teachings can be summed up with this simple yet profound instruction: *But seek first His kingdom and His righteousness.*

TRUE INNER GOODNESS

As Dallas Willard points out in his book *The Divine Conspiracy*, in the Greek, the righteousness Jesus spoke of is not just a set of moral principles, or an ethic of perfection. Jesus' word choice for righteousness could be defined as the quality in people that makes us really right or good—or, in short, "true inner goodness."[4] But it's not our own subjective definition of goodness; rather it is God Himself, the ultimate standard and reality of goodness. He is what we should seek. For in so doing, our innermost being is transformed to a vessel of His true inner goodness.

God's righteousness = true inner goodness

Isn't that what we all long for in our lives? Consider a world where we knew beyond a shadow of a doubt that our government leaders exhibited true inner goodness in their public service, truly being public servants. What would it be like to work for a boss and company that embodied true inner goodness in how they treated employees, vendors, and customers? Imagine a world where advertisers, car sales staff, pastors, priests, roofers, plumbers, the IRS, union bosses, insurance companies, financial advisors, managers, administrators, and anyone else in authority were truly good.

It's hard to think the world could be like this, yet this is the life Jesus sees for us.

In the following pages, I hope to illustrate how radical and relevant these words are for us in the work world. You want your place of work to stand out? Exhibit true inner goodness.

You want to make a difference in the world? True inner goodness is a force to be reckoned with.

Or maybe you simply want to earn a decent living, support your family, and have a clear conscience in doing so? I've yet to come up with anything better than seeking God's kingdom and His true inner goodness.

Can Modern Business Be Righteous?

A part of me wanted to reach across the table and slap the guy upside the head.

I know—neither Christian nor professional on my part. But he deserved it, and it would have felt really good to me. However, I also knew the trials we'd been through together in developing the new gear material that he knew nothing about. We'd saved their company hundreds of thousands of dollars, but he had the audacity to demand price reductions. Around the table, the purchasing managers and I all knew he was bluffing. So, I calmly explained that Edgerton Gear does not charge exorbitant prices and works very hard to offer a fair value to our customers. We raise our prices 3 percent a year to keep up with inflation, in order to keep quality employees, and reinvest in state-of-the-art equipment.

It was obvious he wasn't listening as he repeated his mantra. Either we reduce our prices by 2 percent, or they might go elsewhere. I firmly stated that was not acceptable; the choice of finding another vendor was up to them. I then stood up and walked out of the room.

Halfway down the hall, the head purchasing agent ran after me and excitedly said, "That was awesome! Not one vendor has stood up to him yet. And if you'd have given in to his demands, I would have been really upset."

I asked why, and she replied that it would have shown that Edgerton Gear really wasn't giving their best pricing and that her faith in us was misplaced.

Twenty years later, they're still one of our best customers.

It's often difficult not to be cynical about businesses today, as corruption and greed repeatedly make headlines. For my generation, the Enron scandal of the early 2000s became the poster child of corporate greed, as this energy company was heralded by *Fortune* magazine and named "America's Most Innovative Company" for six consecutive years between 1996 and 2001.[1] At their peak in 2000, their stock price was $90.75, only to plummet to $.67 by early 2002, as the depth and breadth of their corruption and fraud was laid bare. Tens of thousands of employees lost their jobs and their retirement accounts. Rightfully so, some people went to prison.

But the list of companies that self-destructed with corporate greed continued with giants like WorldCom and Lehman Brothers. And it's not just the big dogs and Wall Street that corner the market on excess and lust for more. Local news abounds with stories of embezzlement, fraud, pension funds being raided, and even school booster club funds being stolen by the PTA mom or school volunteer who is the treasurer. Local communities are often decimated by plant closures or downsizing through forced retirements and layoffs.

While market conditions are sometimes a harsh reality—the closing of a printing plant in a digital age, for example—these closures are often difficult to swallow when it's revealed that upper management and CEOs are getting bonuses in the millions of dollars for cutting costs. (Hey buddy, how about cutting your salary and not taking a bonus to save your company money? Ever think of that?)

In fact, in 2014, the average salary of CEOs in the top 400 companies on the S&P was 204 times greater than the average employee's salary. For my company, if a machinist makes $50,000 a year, I would need to take a salary north of $10,000,000, if we abided by that standard.

Four CEOs earned more than a thousand times the median salary of their workforce.[2] I support market capitalism, but this is unthinkably excessive.

Some incredibly wealthy friends of mine might argue that I'm bordering on socialism. However, I read in Scripture that "the love of money is a root of all kinds of evil" (1 Tim. 6:10). The love of money is so prevalent, we think it's normal. What many business leaders fail to comprehend is how their greed impacts the morale of their workforces.

A recent Gallup poll showed that a whopping 87 percent of workers worldwide are not actively engaged in their jobs.[3] What does this mean? Gallup categorized worker engagement on a scale, ranging from actively engaged to actively disengaged. "Actively engaged" describes those workers who are purposely innovative, creative, and bringing their best efforts.

Then there are those who are simply engaged. They do their jobs well, but their creative talents and juices aren't flowing for a variety of reasons, such as lack of appreciation or opportunity.

There are also those who are disengaged, meaning they've pretty much checked out and just going through the motions to earn a paycheck. And finally there are the actively disengaged. Run away from these types, as they hate their jobs, seek ways to be counterproductive, and will take down with them anyone who will listen.

How tragic that 87 percent are not actively engaged! Work has the potential to be a place of tremendous fulfillment, as it allows our God-given creativity and talents to be expressed and appreciated. Yet sadly, this is far from the normal experience in the workplace. For most, it's simply a place to make a living, to earn enough money to go do the things they really want to do. In manufacturing, there is often the sense of just "working for the man," just being a cog in a big machine to make the big fat cats and investors an easy buck.

I don't just dislike what I see in much of business today—I abhor it. It's as if we've been subjects under a tyrannical ruler, where greed, hatred, oppression, selfishness, addiction, boredom, and confusion are normal. Thinking back to the hatchet man who insisted on a 2 percent across-the-board price reduction, it's obvious that business-as-usual for him was bullying and intimidating suppliers. As with many people in the work world, business was a big game, to see who could get the most, no matter the cost in human dignity.

When fear, distrust, and greed rule the business world, creativity is stifled, individualism trumps teamwork, and to quote the old poem about "Casey at the Bat," "There is no joy in Mudville." Work becomes a joyless, tedious job that sucks the best years of life out of us. I've worked for and with too many companies like this. I don't want to be part of that world.

For example, after living in California for a few years in my mid-twenties, I was broke and needed a job ASAP. Although it was the last thing imaginable in my mind, I turned back to the one thing I was good at: being a machinist. Conveniently, there was a machine shop just six blocks from my house that made missile parts for the Tomahawk cruise missile.

Although they weren't hiring, when they found out I was a journeyman machinist from Wisconsin, they hired me on the spot for the graveyard shift. The job turned out to embody the worst stereotypes of manufacturing. It was filthy, disorganized, and demeaning. My job was to grind the fiberglass nose cones for the missiles, and the fiberglass would get into every pore of my body and I'd itch like crazy.

The worst part, however, was my fellow machinists. My foreman was an alcoholic who would leave in the middle of every shift and go to a bar until closing time. One coworker was a drug dealer, while another coworker was a loyal cocaine customer during work hours. The last coworker was belligerent and pompous, bragging to me what a great husband and father he was, even though he left for several hours several nights a week to have an extramarital fling.

Nobody cared about their jobs, and why? Because the company didn't care about them.

It was also well known we were working on a big defense contract and were defrauding the government. After three months of this, I finally quit, and the owners were thrown back in jail for a second time a few years later. There was absolutely no sense of goodness or righteousness in that experience.

So, when I read about Jesus teaching the crowds about "true inner goodness," I begin to understand. Those of us who are working class stiffs are often on the short end of the stick when such inner goodness doesn't exist in the business world.

What is this righteousness? Our first clue might be in Luke 1:12, when an angel appears to an elderly and childless man named Zechariah and tells him that he and his wife, Elizabeth, will have a son they're to name John. He will grow up to be quite a special lad, eventually telling folks to turn from their miserable way of life and live the way that God intended.

John will baptize these people as a symbol of their change (thus the name John the Baptist). As the forerunner of Jesus and actually his cousin, John will "go on before the Lord, in the spirit and power of Elijah, to turn the hearts of the parents to their children and the disobedient to the *wisdom of the righteous*—to make ready a people prepared for the Lord" (Luke 1:17, emphasis added).

It's interesting that the disobedient will be attracted to this wisdom of the righteous. Why? When I think of the "disobedi-ent," I think of the redneck crowd I grew up with here in the Midwest. We could be an unruly bunch, drinking and carousing, being more than a bit sketchy in our language and behavior.

In my small town of five thousand, there have been more bars than gas stations for as long as I can remember. I had friends who would enjoy looking for a fight, and many of us engaged in minor vandalism. As we got older, our toys got more expensive and our behavior moderated, as we had to become somewhat responsible adults. But all in all, in light of God's standards, I think most of us would agree, if we're honest, that the word *disobedient* still fits us.

So why would some brand of righteousness be attractive to us and cause us to turn our lives over to its wisdom? Frankly, we're a defeated and discouraged lot. Life is hard and unfair. As the middle class, we have often been subject to unfair and oppressive job situations. The government doesn't often feel like our friend. Big business, the banks, and the Wall Street brokers seem to make their living off hardworking simpletons like us. We do the grunt work that keeps the lights on and the toilets flushing.

I think of the words of George Bailey in the classic film *It's a Wonderful Life*, when he tells off the evil Mr. Potter who oppresses the working class at every turn and refers to them as "rabble": "Just remember this, Mr. Potter, that this 'rabble' you're talking about, they do most of the working and paying and living and dying in this community."[4]

We're often taken for granted and rarely appreciated. And it's much worse for those we classify as the poor and disenfranchised, who don't have the access

> **Righteousness is *practical* "true inner goodness."**

or the privileges the working class enjoy. So it's fairly easy to be disgruntled, defeated, and discouraged. It could be argued our disobedience is really a reaction to our hopelessness. We long for fairness, truth, purpose, and hope, but we've been let down too many times.

Yet Zechariah is told that his son, John, the soon-to-be Baptist, will come with a message from God that will turn our hearts around, as we won't be able to resist this new wisdom of the righteous. Why?

John grows up to be a rather eccentric type who wears camel

hair for clothes and eats locusts and wild honey. Plain folks are drawn to him as he preaches about God's coming kingdom and a practical righteousness they can relate to.

I imagine he'd fit in well with the biker crowd here in Wisconsin. When asked what they should do so as not to be left out of this kingdom, he responds by telling them to be truly generous, fair, and honest, not just to pretend to be. He openly criticizes the religious elite and government officials for being corrupt and oppressive.

Predictably, he is thrown in prison for doing so and is eventually beheaded. It turns out government officials and the elite don't appreciate having their corruption pointed out. But before he dies, he makes it clear that Jesus is the one everyone should really listen to, that He will usher in a new level of righteousness never seen before.

As Jesus begins His ministry of teaching God's kingdom, healing the sick, and casting out demons, this word *righteousness* repeatedly surfaces. In the Sermon on the Mount, in Matthew 5 and 6 alone, Jesus uses the word five times. He says we should hunger and thirst for it; we should practice it in secret; we will be blessed if we're persecuted because of it; and if ours doesn't surpass that of the Pharisees and teachers of the law, we can't enter His kingdom!

Later on, while teaching at the temple, He tells the religious elite that John came to show them what righteousness is, but they didn't believe Him—though the tax collectors, prostitutes, and the rabble like us did.

So what is it? Again, what is he talking about? Keeping in mind Jesus Himself was a tradesman and grew up in a family business, His message of righteousness is far more relevant than we may have realized.

JOSEPH & SONS HANDCRAFTED PRODUCTS. PLOWS R US

We often hear that Jesus was a carpenter, a trade He learned from his father. This was often the early version of our modern-day apprenticeship. However, it's very likely He wasn't just a simple carpenter in the way people assume.

The word in Greek for carpenter can also mean woodworker, stone mason, iron worker, or builder. A more accurate translation for our contemporary language might be craftsman. It suggests that it was used sometimes for someone who would design and build a boat, or even a plow for farming. It's possible Jesus not only made furniture, spoons, dishes, and the doors, but undertook the designing and building of a house as an entrepreneur.

Given His experience in the family business, I believe it's worth considering what He might have to say about business. What would a Jesus-run business look like? After all, He has more to say about the marketplace than almost any other topic, as His parables and teachings are rich with images of everyday transactions and encounters. He challenged listeners to be virtuous in every aspect of life, including their business dealings.

It can be argued that Jesus was killed because He not only upset the religious elite and weakened their grip on societal power, but also threatened the economic ruling class as well. No one enjoys being told they're greedy, oppressive, and unjust, yet Jesus didn't pull any punches. As in our day, tremendous economic disparity, class conflict, racism, and oppression existed.

Not only were there slaves, the Roman ruling class believed manual labor was beneath them. There was an inherent snobbery toward the working class as second-class citizens. Corruption, bribery, and political favors were the status quo.

So when Jesus came on the scene, He simply pointed out that, from God's perspective, there was nothing healthy in any of this. The ruling elite were so oppressive that society was ripe for revolution, and many thought Jesus would be their leader, their deliverer or, as commonly known, their messiah.

However, rather than a military overthrow, Jesus brought a perspective of truth, justice, love, forgiveness, hope, and goodness. In today's terms, we might call Him a radical activist, but He wasn't out leading demonstrations, doing sit-ins, and leading marches. He was basically saying, "Do you want the world to be a better place? Take a good look at yourself first."

Or to quote one of His well-known statements, "Why do you look at the speck of sawdust in your brother's eye and pay no attention to the plank in your own eye?" (Matt. 7:3).

Reflecting back to my earlier account with our customer's hatchet man, it was hard to swallow his condescending, pompous arrogance when I knew he was making a bundle off of us. But isn't this always the way of the oppressor? To demand more and more, no matter how much you've given and they have already taken?

And I know my everyday examples are nothing compared to what many in Jesus' audience were experiencing. So, while acknowledging how corrupt and dysfunctional the current system was, Jesus announced God had not been blind, passive, or ignorant. The time had come for a major intervention.

God's kingdom was at hand.

THY KINGDOM COME—IN EDGERTON GEAR

My father hated religion. He hated going to church, and it required a monumental effort even to get him through the door for a wedding or funeral. So I'm used to being around people who don't want to go to church. Most of my staff doesn't attend church, and even those who don't vehemently oppose it, as my father did, often don't find church attendance relevant or meaningful.

They're not alone. For years, experts have been examining why church attendance in the US and Canada has been steadily declining. The book *Why Men Hate Going to Church* came out a few years ago. Without joining the debate, if we're to be completely honest and open to self-examination, we need to ask how much of what we have come to define as Christianity is actually biblical and rooted in Jesus' teaching.

I think that very little of what we have come to understand as "going to church" on Sunday mornings actually has a biblical basis. We often say we "go to church," yet how can you go to something you already are? In other words, we don't *go* to church; we *are* the church.

The idea of a "worship service" with a programmed order of songs, liturgy, Scripture readings, sermon, prayer, and perhaps one last song cannot be found in the Bible. Although the Jews had a synagogue, for the first few centuries, followers of Jesus met in homes. There wasn't the professional minister class we consider the norm today. Everyone was expected to participate in these gatherings with a song, prayer, teaching, or a word of encouragement. They supported each other to live out their faith every day of the week, no matter their occupation or station in life.

As a Jew, we know that it was Jesus' custom to visit the

synagogue. He taught, healed, and often had His most dramatic confrontations there with the religious elite. However, most of His teachings and interactions happened during the week in fields, boats, streets, and in the marketplace, rubbing shoulders with folks where they worked, lived, and went about their lives.

I have often wondered what Jesus would think of our version of church today. Would He even go to a church building? Perhaps, but I tend to think we would mostly find Him at the factories, offices, shops, and places where we spend the majority of our lives. I ask these questions not to be combative but to reorient our understanding of His message and teachings.

After my father suddenly and unexpectedly died, I was preparing to give his eulogy. My mother gave me his pocket-sized New Testament that was worn and well read. I was shocked to see all the verses he highlighted and underlined, as well as his notes in the back. We knew he hadn't read it for years, but at one time it was very meaningful to him.

There was something about the man he read about in his Bible—God in the flesh, Jesus of Nazareth—that appealed to him. Just as they did over two thousand years ago, Jesus' words still cut through all the noise, the confusion, the hopelessness, and the futility of life. Why does the church struggle to gather in men like my father?

One of my favorite movies is *The Lion, the Witch and the Wardrobe*,[5] based on C. S. Lewis's Chronicles of Narnia.[6] I have read the books several times. Lewis captures our imagination with the tales of four children in England who find a door to the magical world of Narnia. Written in the 1950s, there was no question of there being evil in the world after the horrors and atrocities of the Second World War.

Within Narnia, there is a constant struggle between good and evil. The Christ figure is Aslan, a majestic lion who rules over his kingdom with truth, justice, and compassion. While he is personally present, his kingdom thrives. In his absence, the evil witch imposes her will on the subjects, and Narnia becomes a never-ending winter, where everything is colorless—only cold, dark grays.

One of the most moving scenes comes when Aslan returns, and with every step, vibrant colors of flowers and life burst forth as he comes to take back his kingdom and set the world aright. It's a powerful picture of Jesus bringing His kingdom to earth. Whether you're a follower of Jesus or not, it's difficult to dispute that our world is in need of a heavy dose of goodness, especially in our business world. Just as Narnia needed Aslan, the workplace needs Jesus to bring a new reality of truth, dignity, and justice.

We're God's agents of true inner goodness in all areas of life.

Jesus makes it clear that we're a key component in ushering in God's kingdom. God doesn't force His will on us but invites us to be His ambassadors—His princes and princesses—to usher in the goodness of His kingdom. It requires our willing response of allegiance and obedience to His rule.

For those willing to throw in their lot with Jesus, "the kingdom is in the hearts of humankind as a new creation (Luke 17:21; Matt. 12:28). It's in the world invisibly as the sway of God's rule in the affairs of people and nations."[7]

It's a strange but wonderful dynamic that, as we seek God's kingdom, we discover we're the vehicle or agent through which it comes.

As with many things in life, we become the embodiment of that which we seek. If we seek peace, we become peacemakers. If we pursue excellence, we somehow become models of excellence to those around us.

I've watched my wife choreograph contemporary worship dances over the years, communicating God's love for His people and creation. In the creative process of matching form and bodily movement to music, she toils and wrestles to somehow express deep meaning through movement. When she finally teaches her creation to her students, it becomes clear that in the process of yearning for and creating the perfect dance, she has become the dance. Her girls are then transformed by her transformation.

Like George Bailey in *It's a Wonderful Life*, we discover we unknowingly helped create that which we deeply longed for.

Over the decades, as I've driven to work each morning, I've prayed the Lord's Prayer found in Matthew 6:9–13 thousands of times. After "Thy kingdom come. Thy will be done" (Matt. 6:9–13 KJV), I simply add, "in Edgerton Gear today." I often joke with our staff amid the day-to-day stress and chaos that I'm glad I'm not in charge, but it's no joke. For over twenty-six years, my quest has been to see what a business would be like if given over to God's kingdom.

As mentioned earlier, I'm still clueless in a lot of ways. But what I have learned is that there are opportunities every single day to be different, to take a stand against the greed and rules of war that pervade our business climate. The key lies in the second half of Jesus' admonition to seek God's kingdom. He attaches the phrase, "and his righteousness."

Those three simple words can change the world.

The Pursuit of Purpose

"If you don't grow, you'll die!"

It wasn't a piece of friendly advice; more like an accusation. The customer was snarly and agitated. It's not that I didn't appreciate that he wanted to give us more work. It was just the amount of work he wanted to give us. We were already working ten to twelve hours a day plus Saturdays. So when I kindly explained to him we were already at capacity, he became angry, almost to the point of viciousness.

I wondered why he was so angry. There was something deeper behind his bitterness.

If we're to examine business through the lens of seeking God's kingdom and the associated true inner goodness, it would first be helpful to consider what business should and should not be.

"IT'S ALL ABOUT THE MONEY"

Have you ever had a friend or family member get caught up in a multilevel, pyramid marketing venture? It begins when they hear about how great some product is. But the real allure is how much money they can make if they become a "distributor." They buy a bunch of inventory, sell it to their friends and relatives, and talk them into becoming distributors, too.

These friends and relatives, in turn, sell to their friends and relatives, who supposedly are so enamored by the product and income potential that they become distributors as well. Eventually, if your friend or relative is successful enough at building their own pyramid, or line, they'll make a fortune just living off the commissions.

The wonderful products of these multilevel ventures range from health and fitness supplements to household products to vacation packages and time shares. Sometimes they really may be great products; other times not so much. My friends who work in sales say this is a marketing model that does have merit, but it rarely produces the income promised.

Personally, I absolutely loathe multilevel marketing for one simple reason: it corrupts relationships. I'm no longer my friend's friend simply because we have something in common and enjoy spending time together. In the eyes of my friend, I'm now a "mark," another person on the list for doing business and making profit.

Some of my salesman friends have explained to me that a good salesman knows how to "work their mark." It means putting in the work to build a relationship with the mark, earn their trust, and finally convince them that you have their best interest in mind as you convince them they need the product you're selling.

Although I've been in business for close to three decades, I guess I'm a lousy salesman, as was my father before me. I hate it when someone tries to convince me to do or buy something I really don't want to do or don't need, and I don't want to be that guy to someone else. It's perhaps the main reason I hate shopping. I feel the life being sucked out of me by advertisers and marketers who are incredibly crafty.

Ever walk into a store to buy a new hunting jacket, only to come out an hour later with a whole shopping cart full of stuff? I have, and it bugs me how gullible I am.

The problem with multilevel marketing and other strategies, in my opinion, is their motive. More often than not, it's all about the money, making a quick buck or even a fortune. Is this how God intended business to be?

Or is business a byproduct of a fallen, corrupt world, and making a buck off your brother is just the way it is?

THE CREATION MANDATE

Most of us are familiar with the Bible's creation story. Whether you believe the biblical version of events or disagree on different interpretations of the Genesis account, the fact remains we're here, the earth is here, and human civilization exists because humans have learned to manipulate the earth's natural resources for their benefit.

All our modern conveniences and necessities exist because we take the stuff of earth and either mine it, grow it, and/or make it. We're doing exactly what God created and instructed us to do in the first chapter of Genesis.

> So God created mankind in his own image, in the image of God he created them; male and female he created them. God blessed them and said to them, "Be fruitful and increase in number; fill the earth and subdue it." (Gen. 1:27–28)

In other words, build a civilization.

In the "Craftsman with Character" class I teach, the founding principle for the curriculum is that every person on the planet has two basic needs beyond food and shelter: purpose and relationship. I argue that without them, there is no drive to exist.

To be human is to need (1) a sense of *purpose* and (2) to be in *relationships* with others.

What is the meaning and purpose of life itself? It's a fundamental question that the human race has been asking for a long, long time. Maybe we should be asking it more often today, when our technological age overwhelms us with choices and opportunities for entertainment and distractions.

I think that once every person reaches the end of life, they begin to reflect on what life is all about. *How did I spend my time? What did I accomplish?* And perhaps the scariest question: *Were the things I devoted my life to really worthy of my devotion?* When a person has no sense of purpose, when life makes no sense and has no meaning, it must be a terrible reckoning.

Along with a need for purpose, there's perhaps an even

greater need for relationship. It seems to be true not just for humanity but for all God's creatures. With the numerous farm animals we've raised over the years, we've observed that the animal's greatest need, besides food and water, is to not be alone. Separate a cow, chicken, goat, turkey, or duck from the herd or flock and it will suffer tremendously and often throw a fit.

Recently, one of my beef calves got through the electric fence and was separated from his best friend all night. When I went down to do chores the next morning, there he was on the outside of the barn with a confused and forlorn look on his face. Like a lost puppy, he followed me around the side of the barn to the gate. When I opened the gate, he ran straight into the barn to find his buddy, and his world was right again.

Isolate a human being and you'll break one's spirit. It's no wonder that solitary confinement has always been a powerful form of punishment and torture. We need each other. We can have a tremendous sense of purpose and giftedness, coming up with a cure for cancer, composing a song or dance that makes us weep, building a Fortune 500 company, or being a movie star or athlete—but if we don't have someone to share it with, what does it matter?

Reading the creation account from Eugene Peterson's more earthy paraphrase, *The Message*, we can't help but notice God's intent that we would share—with God and each other—a grand sense of purpose and relationship:

God spoke: "Let us make human beings in our image, make them reflecting our nature. So they can be responsible for the fish in the sea, birds in the air, the cattle, and, yes, Earth itself, and every animal that moves on the face of Earth." God created human beings; he created them godlike. Reflecting God's nature. He created them male and female.

God blessed them: "Prosper! Reproduce! Fill Earth! Take charge! Be responsible for fish in the sea and birds in the air, for every living thing that moves on the face of Earth."

Then God said, "I've given you every sort of seed-bearing plant on Earth and every kind of fruit-bearing tree, given them to you for food. To all animals and all birds, everything that moves and breathes, I give whatever grows out of the ground for food." And there it was.

God looked over everything he had made; it was so good, so very good! (Gen. 1:26–31)

What you've just read has been called the Creation Mandate. We have a tremendous responsibility not only to survive but thrive as stewards of creation. Think of it as God's huge but unfinished science project. He got things started by creating matter from nothing and formed it into planets and stars. He delighted in our planet, and used His infinite creativity to think up such wonders as plants, trees, flowers, fish, all sorts of animals, and a variety of minerals and substances that could be manipulated for useful things, such as pottery and tools.

And just for the sheer joy of it, He left it unfinished so that his most prized creation—our species, humanity—could share in the joy of creating, building, managing, inventing, classifying, organizing, producing, experimenting, and all the other roles needed to make civilization.

I think of when my boys were growing up and wanted to

help me on the farm or in the garden. I'd leave certain projects or chores unfinished, so they could experience the joy of contributing. In their small, limited selves, they were like me and had ideas and questions as they learned new skills and how to interact with their environment.

So it is with us and God. He has given us all the raw materials, along with His talents and creativity, to share in the joy of shaping our world. The vast science project is there for us to pitch in on creating; billions of us are needed to fulfill our roles. Not one of us is identical. Each of us has our unique gifts and talents to contribute to the party. Business is a very important way we fulfill the creation mandate.

A GIFT OF GOD'S GRACE

Jeff Van Duzer addresses the role of business in the grand scheme of God's intent for us to fill the world and make it fruitful:

> First, business appears to be uniquely well situated to work the fields, to cause the land to be fruitful, and to fill the earth . . . "to create wealth." Second, business is also the dominant institution . . . equipped to provide organized opportunities for meaningful and creative work.[1]

Purpose and relationship: they go hand in hand in successful businesses. It's so obvious that we might miss it. Without a meaningful purpose (that is, a needed product or service in the marketplace) and quality relationships working together to provide the product or service, the business is not sustainable.

These two elements alone can be fairly accurate predictors

of whether a business sinks or swims. Think of businesses that were a flash in the pan, or may even have established themselves successfully, then failed. The reason often boils down to one of two factors: either their product or service was no longer needed or relevant, or there was a breakdown in the relationships among the staff, the vendors, and the customers.

With the invention of the automobile, the horse-drawn carriage became obsolete, and the industry collapsed. Kerosene lamps were replaced by electric light bulbs. Restaurants with lousy food or service usually don't last long. My sister, a travel agent, provides fabulous service, but she has struggled to keep her business afloat given the ease of booking travel online. In my industry, I can think of numerous small manufacturing shops that no longer exist because of poor customer service, obsolete equipment and processes, or terrible management that alienated their staff and customers.

> **Our workplace *should be* a place of purpose and quality relationships.**

This is a radical departure from how most people view business, but it's not just about making money. In fact, money isn't even the main motivation. Or at least, it shouldn't be. It's about fulfilling our role in building civilization so people can thrive.

Our little gear shop contributes to the existence of modern civilization in more ways than can be comprehended. Almost every aluminum can, paper cup, and cardboard box in the entire world is made by machinery that uses our gears. Our three customers that make these machines are advanced in their technology and innovation; their machines are sold to customers worldwide who make over 90 percent of the world's cans, cups, and boxes. And these are just three of our customers.

All the modern conveniences we take for granted, such as toilet paper, copy paper, paper towels, sofas, recliners, socks, toothbrushes, light bulbs, shopping carts, paper clips, microwave ovens, espresso machines, and even our smartphones and laptops would not exist without gears.

When pastors or theologians put a higher priority on their work as ministers than on the average trade worker, manufacturer, logger, or truck driver, I gently (and sometimes not so gently) remind them that their Bibles, internet, church buildings with sound systems and screens would not exist without the symphony of the marketplace and the people fulfilling their occupations with skill, creativity, and discipline to make all these goods and services magically appear.

When I speak to students on the value and meaning of work, they're usually terribly ignorant of the complexity, wonder, and necessity of the marketplace. Obviously, I'm a bit partial to manufacturing, so I ask the students to identify any man-made object in the room. I can then illustrate the countless jobs it takes to get that object to our classroom. Scoffing at my challenge, they typically select a simple object like a pencil or piece of paper or a napkin. The conversation goes something like this.

I say, "What is this piece of paper made of?"

"Trees," they answer, as if mine was an exceedingly dumb question.

"How do you start the process of making a tree into paper?"

"You have to cut it down."

"With what?"

"A chainsaw?"

"What's a chainsaw made of?"

The light bulbs start to turn on in their brains. "Steel, plastic, gas, oil, copper for the motor, etcetera."

"So let's start with the steel. Where does that come from?"

"From iron ore and other materials." They're starting to get a clue.

"How do you get the ore out of the ground?"

"You mine it, with earth movers and other heavy equipment."

Anticipating my endless questioning, they will often chime in, ". . . that are made of steel, rubber, and hundreds of other components."

"Now you're starting to get the idea! And we haven't even gotten our tree out of the woods yet to the paper mill!"

If I haven't broken their minds by this point, we further discuss the process of making paper.

As Van Duzer points out, the marketplace has a miraculous quality to it that, he argues, is a form of God's grace. It's worth bearing in mind that work is not an invention of the human species or the animal kingdom. We often view it as something to dread, to be free of, and to get out of. But the ability and desire to work is a tremendous gift that should minister to the soul's need for purpose and relationship. It's part of the DNA God imparted to us. As John Dalla Costa proposes in *Magnificence at Work: Living Faith in Business*,

> Work has always been the locus of God's calling. It would be surprising if it were not, for work matters profoundly as a creative act, as a contribution to sustenance and community, as a mark of human dignity and personal identity."[2]

BUSINESS REFLECTS OUR HEART CONDITION

So the idea is that business is God's instrument to help the world prosper and thrive. But that's far from what most have experienced. In fact, business can actually be blamed for many of our woes, and rightfully so.

The Bible teaches that we're a fallen people who rejected God's good intentions for us by rejecting God Himself. Regardless of your interpretation of the account of the Garden of Eden, there is little doubt that humankind has an amazing capacity for evil on a grand scale, as demonstrated by the atrocities of war throughout history.

Business should be more than just about making money.

Furthermore, the damage done to cultures, tribes, communities, and the environment in the name of business has more horror stories that we can count. As Spider-Man tells us, with much power comes much responsibility. Although business has the power to do tremendous good, it has perhaps even more power to do untold harm. Without naming names, we can all think of corporations that have ravaged the environment, displaced people, and devastated communities by unjust, manipulative, and greedy business practices.

But behind these corporations are real people with real personal lives. Evil doesn't start at the corporate level; it begins in the heart and is very personal. If we want to blame or give credit to business for good or evil, the blame or credit needs to go to the actual people making the decisions that run these businesses.

Wouldn't it be fascinating if Jesus could sit in corporate

boardrooms today? Imagine the scene: the discussion flows around the table about maximizing profit at the expense of a farmer's livelihood or the environment, or the effect on a community by relocating jobs. The legal beagles give their input about making sure the letter of the law is followed as the line of integrity and goodness is blurred.

Having enough of this charade of being "good" because no laws were technically broken, Jesus responds as He did to the Pharisees, who were also more concerned about being legally correct while skirting the law of love:

> "Frauds! Isaiah's prophecy of you hit the bull's-eye: These people make a big show of saying the right thing, but their heart isn't in it. They act like they're worshiping me, but they don't mean it. They just use me as a cover for teaching whatever suits their fancy." (Matt. 15:9 MSG)

Calling out their less than ethical thinking and behavior, far from exhibiting true inner goodness in their business decisions and dealings, Jesus continues His tirade, mincing no words (according to Peterson's paraphrase, at least):

> "Are you being willfully stupid? Don't you know that anything that is swallowed works its way through the intestines and is finally defecated? But what comes out of the mouth gets its start in the heart. It's from the heart that we vomit up evil arguments, murders, adulteries, fornications, thefts, lies, and cussing." (Matt. 15:16–19 MSG)

Repeating Van Duzer's assertion that businesses should (1) "provide the community with goods and services that will enable it to flourish, and (2) . . . provide opportunities for meaningful work that will allow employees to express their God-given creativity,"[3] it's imperative we not lose sight of the fact that, for the follower of Jesus, business done the kingdom way starts and ends as a matter of the heart.

It's doing the right thing for all involved as much as possible. As business leaders and owners, we can't expect our businesses to be ethical and good if we're personally greedy, selfish, and corrupt. Nor can we expect a higher standard from our staff. Only by taking an honest, hard look in the mirror can we come to understand how business can be an instrument through which God's kingdom brings healing and restoration to a fallen world.

Our businesses are a reflection and extension of who we are. Jesus doesn't mince words; a clean exterior can hide our filthy insides for only so long. Consider Jesus' words to the religious professionals who worked hard at keeping up appearances of being "holy."

"You're hopeless, you religion scholars and Pharisees [and business leaders]! Frauds! You burnish the surface of your cups and bowls so they sparkle in the sun, while the insides are maggoty with your greed and gluttony. Stupid Pharisee! Scour the insides, and then the gleaming surface will mean something.

"You're hopeless, you religion scholars and Pharisees! Frauds! You're like manicured grave plots, grass clipped and the flowers bright, but six feet down its all rotting bones and worm-eaten flesh. People look at you and think you're saints, but beneath the skin you're total frauds." (Matt. 23:25–28 MSG)

Doing business the kingdom way is, therefore, an expression of the soul's desire to give glory and credit to God for His grace, compassion, and goodness in our lives. It's not just about making a buck or a fortune. Business is, or at least should be, our attempt to use all the gifts and talents God bestowed on us to contribute to the greater good.

BUSINESS AS USUAL, OR REACHING FOR MORE?

At this point, you may be wondering whether I'm some idealistic airhead with my head in the clouds. Over the years, my own staff has wondered the same thing, as have my wife, my parents, friends, and to be honest, myself as well. For whatever reason, I've always been a bit obsessed and more than intrigued with the ideal and perfect life, not the way things are but how they were supposed to be.

Maybe it's a remnant of our ancestors before we became the fallen people we are—a whispering in our souls that things aren't as they should be, as God's Spirit woos and coaxes us to His higher plane. I truly believe the longing for meaning, depth, and harmony is in all of us. But life has beaten us down, hardened our hearts and made us more than a bit cynical that such a life could actually exist, that business could be as I'm proposing. We've settled for defeat and a way of living that is far less than what God intended. But deep inside, don't we all want life to be more and not just have more as in stuff, power, prestige, and comfort?

As Dalla Costa reminds us, "Wanting to be more than we

are is a completely human aspiration, driving much of what we understand as social progress and economic development. It's also the restlessness to be expected among the children of God."[4]

When my parents started Edgerton Gear in 1962, it was not out of an ideal notion to touch the world. As with most businesses, it was out of necessity. Being dirt poor, with three daughters under the age of seven and a son on the way, putting food on the table was my dad's first priority. He had no lofty notions of being a light in the community or in industry. Those ideas would have all been mumbo jumbo to him.

My mother would tell me she'd often pray for a farmer to come to the shop with a broken implement that needed immediate fixing. Hopefully, the farmer would pay cash and my mother could then buy groceries on the way home for dinner. This can be the stark reality of being in business for entrepreneurs and small business owners. We need to make a profit to make a decent living. If we don't, the alternative is gut-wrenching.

The struggle of making payroll, paying vendors, and getting customers who pay on time is our world. For the first seven years of Edgerton Gear, my dad never took a vacation and often went on the road during the day to look for work. Then, if he did find work for the shop, he'd stay late into the night to deliver the parts back to the customer as soon as possible to get paid to feed his family.

The sacrifices both he and my mom made to establish the business are very meaningful to me. It was hard, and I think only others who have had to start businesses can truly understand and appreciate what they endured. However, although my dad wouldn't have picked up a book like this, he embodied the practical reality of what I believe God intended business to be. Either because of his intuition or survival skills, he laid a foundation of the three ideals of quality, value, and service.

He had a vision that for business to survive and thrive, it needed to reach for the ideal. In the cutthroat world of the marketplace, virtuous business practices set it apart from others. The practical side of true inner goodness has no greater relevance than the matter of money and profit.

Money and Profit

His company was working seven days a week for months on end, and he expected the same from us.

Our sales had been growing at 10 to 20 percent annually for the past five years. So when he said, "If you don't grow, you die," he either didn't understand me, or he wasn't listening.

I tried to explain that we were indeed growing—we just didn't want to grow out of control.

For him, it was all about the money and taking in as much work as he could, no matter the toll it was taking on him, his staff, or his vendors like us. It clearly ticked him off that we didn't want to play along with his obsession. We were all exhausted and overwhelmed. What was the point of it all?

If you're a linear thinker like I am, it may seem illogical to talk about money and profit this early in the book. So far, all we've discussed is having a calling to business, how God has a different plan for how we do business, and that God's righteousness, His true inner goodness, should be the basis for how we conduct our businesses.

Wouldn't the next logical step be to discuss how to start a business or at least come up with a business plan, and all the facets of production, supply chain, marketing, sales, and human resources? Aren't we getting ahead of ourselves talking about money and profit?

I couldn't agree more, but at the same time, I argue that if we don't first have our heads screwed on straight when it comes to money, going into business will be like walking into a minefield without a metal detector. With every step of your business plan, a wrong relationship with money can potentially blow up everything you've worked for and all your good intentions. Even worse, before you know it, you'll find your life is far from what God intended.

Make no mistake about it. Business either survives or dies based on profit. We can't live without it, but there is nothing else in the entire universe that has such a corrupting power to destroy us.

Think I'm being a bit overdramatic? Take a minute to consider the effect money has on people. There is an addictive quality to it, and I'm not just talking about the gambler at the craps table or playing the slots. Have you ever loaned money to a friend or relative, been in a dispute over a will, or bought lottery tickets when the jackpot is in the hundreds of millions? We're all tempted by money, and we daydream of what life could be like if we had an unlimited supply of it.

However, winners of the lottery often tell stories about how they wished they had never won. Young star athletes who sign huge contracts often end up broke, and they self-destruct. Pick up a Hollywood tabloid and you can't help but be awed by how weird some celebrities become because their wealth allows them to be.

Business people are no different, or maybe even worse, because in the unmerciful marketplace, at the end of the day, we're solely judged on whether we made a profit. We may have a wonderful product that truly serves humanity, feeds the starving children, and has almost no carbon footprint. But the banks, vendors, and employees don't care about our good intentions if we can't pay our bills.

We have to make a profit. However, at what point do we cross the line of becoming greedy about that profit? Is there such a line? Is there such a thing as a fair profit, or is any profit acceptable as long as someone is willing to pay? When it comes to pricing structures, is the best criterion "whatever the market will bear"?

Consider it from a kingdom perspective. Is profit a necessary evil, filthy lucre that soils our hands and hearts, or is there a righteous way to handle it that reflects our true inner goodness?

I'm convinced that how we answer these questions about profit has more bearing on laying the foundation for our businesses than we realize. And it all starts with our own personal relationship with money.

THE PRICE TAG ON "HAPPY"

In our "Craftsman with Character" class, we show the thought-provoking documentary *The Happy Movie*[1] because it explores what makes humans around the globe happy. The prevalent notion that money makes us happy is honestly examined. Most of us know that's a myth, yet much of our lives are spent in the pursuit of it just the same.

In the movie, many people are asked what would or does make them happy. Not surprisingly, the most popular response is money. So, the question is asked whether money really makes us happy or whether we all believe a lie. The research showed that the difference in happiness for the homeless person making nothing at all versus earning $50,000 a year is huge.

Common sense tells us we need our basic needs met: food, shelter, and clothing. The misery of living on the streets without them can be greatly alleviated with enough money to purchase these necessities. So in a sense, money can indeed help us be "happy." As our income grows, we can afford healthier food, nicer clothes, and better shelter.

However—and this is a big however—the research shows that the difference between happiness for those making $50,000 and those making $50 million a year is minimal. In fact, the research suggests that as one becomes wealthy, happiness actually starts to decrease. Money becomes the goal rather than the means to other goals, and once that happens, something isn't right.

Most of us who didn't grow up in a wealthy home learned money was hard to come by, and we often wished for more of it. As we got older, having more money actually did have an effect on our happiness, as we were able to buy more modern conveniences, eat out more, take an annual vacation, and simply not worry so much about making ends meet.

However, we also were seduced into thinking that if having some money made us happy, it stood to reason that having more of it would make us even happier. This logic eventually leads to the belief that if we have lots and lots of money, we will have lots and lots of happiness, which simply isn't true. More money doesn't mean more happiness. Rather, it can actually spell misery.

In simple terms, at what point, instead of owning our toys, do our toys start owning us?

And what does this have to do with profit in our businesses?

Consider that famous Bible verse we've already mentioned: "For the love of money is a root of all kinds of evil. Some people, eager for money, have wandered from the faith and pierced themselves with many griefs" (1 Tim. 6:10).

It's nothing new to point out that money itself isn't the root of evil, but the love of it is what gets us into trouble. It simply can't be our main objective. As Paul Stevens has said, in business, profit is like blood to the body. The body needs blood to live, but the body doesn't live just to make blood.[2]

Profit is like blood to the body. We can't live without it but making money is not our main purpose.

This is an important point. Can you imagine if the reason we took care of our bodies was just to make more blood? We'd live for nothing else, and it would be absurd, but this is exactly how many people in business think of money. Business should be about providing the community with goods and services, and creating opportunities for meaningful work to help people express their creativity. But too many people exist simply to make money, and their business practices often reflect this.

Recently, I helped my mother purchase a new car. We spent two hours with a salesman at a dealership, and he seemed to sincerely care about helping my mother find a safe, reliable vehicle, suitable for our Wisconsin winters. She was trading in my recently deceased father's larger vehicle and wanted something a bit smaller and more manageable.

Purposefully dressed in my shop clothes so as not to tip my hand that I was the president of our company, I looked the part of a simple machinist, while my mother looked the part of a gullible, senior-aged lady. After she selected the vehicle and features she wanted, the salesman worked up his offer as well as the trade-in value of my father's vehicle.

I was stunned. The salesman was not only several thousand dollars low for the trade-in value but several thousand dollars high on the new vehicle. With the tools available on the internet, it's easy for anyone to determine fair market prices, and yet he assumed neither my mother nor I were tech savvy. He tried to gouge us for every penny he could.

I took out my smartphone and slid it across the desk to him, along with my business card that showed I was a company president. The phone showed the Kelly Blue Book value of my mother's vehicle. Suddenly he was speechless. I threw his offer back on his desk and stated that his offer was insulting, as it appeared he viewed us as an unsophisticated woman with her simpleton shop-boy-of-a-son. He stammered and tried to salvage the situation by saying he had to start negotiations somewhere.

We tried another dealership the next day, where we had just the opposite experience. The salesman also seemed to sincerely care, but when he got down to pricing both the trade-in and the new vehicle, his offer was actually more than $4,000 lower than the previous dealer's. He sought out every company discount without being prompted. It was obvious his first priority wasn't to make as much money as possible but to serve us and win a loyal customer.

If we love money and believe it's the answer to our woes and trials, our motivations for doing business righteously with true inner goodness will be compromised. As Jesus said, "Watch out! Be on your guard against all kinds of greed; life does not consist in an abundance of possessions" (Luke 12:15).

GOD OR MAMMON

Growing up in rural Wisconsin had its advantages, one of which was *not* being surrounded by opulent wealth. The majority of the folks in our town were the blue-collar working class. Even wealthy bankers, doctors, and lawyers seemed like ordinary people by our standards. They may have had more stuff than the rest of us, but we still rubbed elbows with them at school events, the bowling alley, and the hardware stores, sharing hunting and fishing stories.

So when I arrived in Orange County, California, in the mid-1980s as a starving student and athlete, I saw wealth on a level I had never imagined. I eventually landed a job as a pastor to college students in a megachurch in Newport Beach. On Sundays, the parking lot was full of BMWs, Mercedes Benzes, Jaguars, and every other ultra-expensive status vehicle of wealth.

During the school year, most of my students were from the University of California-Irvine or various small colleges in the area. But during the summer, the children of the super wealthy who attended the church would come home for three months while the other students would return to their home towns.

It's hard to describe how drastically different my small congregation of college students would be when this seasonal change happened. Yes, they were all just people, but I soon began to take pity on the students from the wealthy families. Their problems and pressures were far greater than the "average" students. The peer pressure to keep up appearances of looking beautiful and wealthy was tremendous. The incidents of drug and alcohol abuse, bulimia, anorexia, parents who were divorced or having affairs, and other struggles far outnumbered those of the average students.

Being a pastor on staff, I also had an inside look into the lives of many "successful" and super wealthy business people. I couldn't help but conclude that being very wealthy was something I never wanted to be. Handling large sums of money was a tremendous responsibility, and few seemed to handle it well.

Years later, as my wife and I were preparing to return to Edgerton Gear, it occurred to me that the business had the potential to be more successful than it had been. What if it made a lot of money? Would we become miserable like so many of the wealthy I knew in Southern California? Would wealth entangle and ensnare us?

I decided we needed a plan before we left for Wisconsin, and I did an independent study at Regent College on the topic of money. Twenty-five years later, one thought still stands out from that study, which has guided pretty much every financial business decision since. It's a radical concept that you may agree with—a guiding principle that has worked for me.

Some have argued I'm too extreme, but based on what I've seen and experienced when it comes to money, I'd rather err on the side of caution. Simply put, money is not just a neutral means of exchange, but a power more potent and dangerous than unstable nitroglycerin.

Consider Jesus' words: "You can't worship two gods at once.

Loving one god, you'll end up hating the other. Adoration of one feeds contempt for the other. You can't worship God and Money both" (Matt. 6:24 MSG).

God and money are referred to as gods that are worshiped or adored. We're faced with a choice of which one we will serve or worship. We can't have it both ways, loving them both equally. They're in conflict with each other, both competing for our affections. It's like being caught in a love triangle or forced to choose between friends who hate each other. But it's much worse than that because, from Jesus' kingdom perspective, only one truly has our best interest at heart, while the other wants to enslave and ultimately destroy us.

Jacques Ellul, the French historian and theologian, was the first to introduce me to this perspective in *Money & Power*. The entire book is a masterful analysis of defining money and power, and the role they play in our modern societies, as well as their effect on our spiritual health. He points out that in the above Scripture, Jesus uses the familiar Aramaic word *mammon*, which can also be translated "wealth." But what is unusual is that Jesus "personifies money and considers it a sort of a god . . . [it] claims divinity . . . [and] reveals something exceptional about money, for Jesus did not usually use deifications and personifications."[3]

In other words, money is not just an inanimate object we use. "What Jesus is revealing is that money is a power . . . Money is not a power because man uses it, because it's the means of wealth or because accumulating money makes

> **"What Jesus is revealing is that money is a power."**
> —*Jacques Ellul*

things possible. It's a power before all that."[4]

I never used to think of money as a power or deity, as something that is competing with God for my allegiance, but common sense and experience tells me this rings true. The only other power I can think of that has the capacity to grab hold of us and make us obsessive is lust, but not even lust can convince us that it's the answer to all of our troubles in the way money can.

As Ellul argues, Jesus "is speaking of a power which tries to be like God, which makes itself our master and which has specific goals."[5]

GREED IS GOOD?

Greed is rampant, not only in our culture, but in the history of the world. We marvel at the ridiculous extremes people have reached to attain wealth. In the Dutch Tulip Bulb craze of the 1600s, speculators drove up the price of tulip bulbs to insane levels. "In 1633, a single bulb of Semper Augustus was already worth . . . enough to feed, clothe and house a whole Dutch family for half a lifetime, or sufficient to purchase one of the grandest homes on the most fashionable canal in Amsterdam for cash, complete with a coach house and an 80-foot garden."[6] What drove this? Greed.

My great-great uncle was supposedly murdered by his mining partner in northern California over their claim during the gold rush. Like countless other examples, the reason is greed.

Of course, the argument could be made that greed is good. I still remember watching the 1987 movie *Wall Street*, when the character Gordon Gekko gives the convincing speech that, "Greed, for lack of a better word, is good . . . [It]captures the essence of the evolutionary spirit. Greed, in all of its forms; greed for life, for money, for love, [for] knowledge has marked the upward surge of mankind."[7]

It's an honest and compelling statement as it can easily be argued that America's rise as a superpower is a tale of the fruitfulness of greed. From exploring and settling the early frontiers, to the innovations of the industrial revolution, all were driven by humanity's insatiable appetite to "strike it rich." The epic careers of Rockefeller, Carnegie, J. P. Morgan, Edison, Ford, and others are heroic tales of the competitive drive to win and be wealthy. It's hard to fathom what our modern civilizations would be without their contributions to the railroad, gas, oil, steel, electricity, and automobile industries.

Just the changes within my own lifetime are amazing. My children have never known a world without Microsoft, Apple, or Google. Would any of these technologies exist without the underlying greed that surely fueled their innovations?

So how do we live in a world where money and greed rule? The question is so complex, it's impossible to come up with a simple answer. Money is so interwoven into every aspect of our businesses that it's impossible to be in business without it. So do we all cloister ourselves away in monasteries and become monks and nuns, away from the filthy world of business?

One of the most compelling reasons I decided to follow Jesus was how rooted His teaching is in reality, fully recognizing our world is really messed up. I remember reading John 16:33 for the first time, "In this world you will have trouble." Yep, that pretty much summed up my life up to that point.

However, He continues by saying, "But take heart! I have overcome the world." The verb tense says the overcoming has taken place. Yet we find ourselves squarely in the middle of the now and the not yet. His kingdom is here now, coming through us, but it has not yet been fully accomplished.

Consider D-Day, when the Allied forces stormed the beaches of Normandy. The Allies had overcome the world of Fortress Europe. It was the beginning of the end for the Nazis, but there was a lot of bloody fighting yet to be done. God is in the process of taking back this planet, but there's a lot of work yet in front of us.

In the midst of our current messed up reality, He gives us a vision of what could and will be. His righteousness, His true inner goodness, sets a new standard of how life was meant to be. So, although money is necessary in business, it doesn't have to rule over us. Jesus is refreshingly blunt: we can't serve both God and money. We will either adore one and hate the other or vice versa.

It's a battle and a choice we face countless times every day.

RICH TOWARD GOD

Jesus fully recognizes our battles and temptations. In Luke 12, He is surrounded by thousands who are hanging on His every word, because of His profound wisdom and teachings about everyday life. He paints for them a word picture of what His kingdom looks like.

Suddenly, someone in the crowd asks Jesus to settle a dispute. The guy's brother is in control of their family inheritance and isn't sharing. Not getting the gist of the kingdom message and more concerned about his personal finances, he tells Jesus to make his brother share.

I picture one of my sons as a little boy, screaming at me that his brothers aren't sharing. Jesus handles the situation much better than I've done with my sons. His reply? "Mister, what makes you think it's any of my business to be a judge or mediator for you?"

Then He says to them, "Take care! Protect yourself against the least bit of greed. Life is not defined by what you have, even when you have a lot" (Luke 12:14–15 MSG).

And with that, He tells the story of a wealthy farmer with abundant crops. The harvest is so good, he decides to build bigger barns and store the surplus. He'll be set for life, ready to eat, drink, and be merry. At this point, however, God shows up and says, "Fool! Tonight you die. And your barnful of goods—who gets it?"

Jesus basically concludes, "That's what happens when you fill your barn with Self and not with God" (vv. 16–21). Other translations refer to this as "not being rich toward God."

I'm part of a lineage that has struggled with alcohol abuse, and I'm fully aware that if I play with fire, I'm going to get burned. My wife and sons hold me accountable to certain parameters. I'm prone to addiction and excess. I've learned and am still learning I need boundaries, rules, and strict guidelines to keep me from going off the path.

So when Jesus personifies mammon as a competing god, a legitimate power that competes for my allegiance, my strategy is to have mechanisms in my life that test my allegiance to God.

EXCESS PROFIT

One of the most challenging aspects of profit concerns what to do with it. There is, of course, the constant need to reinvest back into the company by updating equipment and tooling. Otherwise, I used to believe the simple answer was to give it to the employees.

Our businesses obviously need competent and talented people. Without them, our businesses would not exist. Although money is not at the top of any survey related to job satisfaction, if we don't at least offer a competitive wage for our industry, the best and brightest will go elsewhere.

What I didn't anticipate (but should have) is what happens when a workforce is given every opportunity to be successful, given the freedom to be innovative and productive, and within an environment that is empowering and affirming. If the business model is sound, it's not uncommon for profits to rise. It stands to reason that employees should share in the bounty through some form of bonuses and profit sharing, which many businesses today wisely do.

However, the reality is that we can't expect our staff to share our convictions about disarming the power of money. Many of them may not be living within their means, no matter how much they're paid. Some may be caught in the lie mentioned earlier: that more money means more happiness.

We're all bombarded by media messages and advertisers saying that the "good life" can be bought. As business owners, then, we can easily perpetuate the lie and obsession for more if we communicate that money is our top priority. Profit and bonuses may be rewards for our efforts. They're cause for celebration but not our main motivation. We must be vigilant in keeping money in its proper place.

So what do we do with excess profit or excess money? Maybe the mortgage is paid off and our kids are done with college or tech school, and we suddenly inherit a small fortune, or get an unexpected large bonus at work. Do we just spend it on ourselves, or are there deeper considerations? I hardly know of any other question that requires more prayer for wisdom and discernment than the prayer for courage to be obedient to the answers. I don't know of any other power that changes relationships and corrupts people and organizations like money. Whether it's a friend who suddenly views me as a potential client for life insurance, dietary supplements, knives, or household goods, or a business owner who is either desperate for money or has too much of it, I'm always amazed at how money changes people.

This convinces me that Ellul is right about Jesus' teaching on God and mammon. Money has a tremendous power to entice and corrupt. It must be approached with equal doses of wisdom, discernment, humility, and courage.

Frank Hanna, a successful entrepreneur and thought leader on the topic of wealth and philanthropy, is tremendously helpful in framing the discussion on wealth. In his book *What Your Money Means and How to Use It Well*, Hanna tackles the question of how much money is enough. Since the answer is different for everyone, Hanna proposes that we begin by asking, "Do we have enough for the bare necessities? Not just for ourselves but for all those who depend on us?"[8]

How much money is enough?

Again, since the answer will be different for everyone, Hanna helps us define our bare necessities by asking, "How much do I need just to keep myself and my dependents alive, with absolutely nothing left over?"[9] Hanna does not suggest this is the level we should aspire to, but simply asks the question to help us distinguish between bare necessities and genuine needs.

Food, water, shelter, and clothing qualify as bare necessities.

I think of prisoners of war who are barely kept alive. The poor and destitute may have the bare necessities, but this is hardly the life God intended.

Like a loving parent, God doesn't just want us to survive but to flourish and have every opportunity to live up to our potential. So, the next question Hanna asks is what are our needs beyond our bare necessities that enable us to flourish? He defines this next level of need as genuine needs. "Genuine needs are the things a person must have in order to develop as he/she should, physically, morally, intellectually, and spiritually."[10]

> **"Genuine needs are the things a person must have in order to develop as he/she should, physically, morally, intellectually, and spiritually."**
> —*Frank Hanna*

Although how we define genuine needs will again vary greatly, I think we all can agree some universal genuine needs would be nutritious food, a loving and supportive home, quality education, quality healthcare, and access to meaningful employment.

However, my particular genuine needs may seem ridiculously luxurious to a family in rural Honduras or in the ghettos of Accra, Ghana. In rural Wisconsin, there is no public transportation such as I've seen in Honduras, where public buses go to many remote villages.

So we have a genuine need of personal transportation. For my industry, a genuine need is a technical college education. For teachers in the United States, a credentialed college education is a genuine need. To grow our businesses, capital to purchase essential equipment and hire competent staff is a genuine need. As equipment ages and as more efficient technologies become available, reinvestment back into the company is a genuine need. Providing healthcare for our staff as well as a secure future is a genuine need.

All of the above are good uses for our profits, and require much discernment and wisdom as we determine how much to spend on each of them.

After constantly juggling all the genuine needs, we may discover there is rarely any excess profit left. However, if our businesses are successful, there will inevitably come a time when we're actually faced with the blessing and curse of not knowing what to do with our profits.

Hanna defines this as nonessential wealth. This is where things can get especially dicey, fraught with land mines.

NONESSENTIAL WEALTH

Hanna explores numerous ways we can spend our *nonessential wealth*, such as giving it to charity, spending it on ourselves, and leaving it to our children. He rightly recognizes that "*nonessential wealth* can be volatile and dangerous—so much so that it may seem literally better to burn it than to let it remain in our own hands or let it fall into the hands of those we love."[11]

We all know children who are spoiled, those children who are given every imaginable toy and latest gadget. Many of us see nothing wrong with lavishing our children with gifts, but we do them a tremendous disservice when we teach them they're the center of the universe and are entitled to anything they want.

I don't know whether boomers are the worst that have ever

lived when it comes to developing our children's character, but based on personal experience and the media, we have to rank near the bottom. We seem to think the more we give our children in terms of stuff and the alleviation of struggles, the better we are as parents. On the contrary, it can be argued we're actually doing incredible harm. Who actually wants their children to be selfish, lazy, spoiled, unmotivated, antisocial, and ungrateful?

> **"Character cannot be developed in ease and quiet. Only through experience of trial and suffering can the soul be strengthened, ambition inspired, and success achieved."**
> —*Helen Keller*

Yet when we shield them from natural consequences of bad behavior and do not allow them to struggle, we're often creating little monsters. Quoting Helen Keller, Hanna points out wealth can impede character development: "Character cannot be developed in ease and quiet. Only through experience of trial and suffering can the soul be strengthened, ambition inspired, and success achieved."[12]

Wealth has incredible power to do good things, but even more power to be harmful. In business, it's essential we recognize these two sides of wealth, pray for wisdom and humility, and remember who the wealth actually belongs to. If we begin to think that we've done everything by ourselves, and that we deserve to be rich, then we've taken a wrong turn. As Moses warned the Israelites, "Remember the LORD your God, for it is he who gives you the ability to produce wealth" (Deut. 8:17–18).

STRATEGIES THAT WORK FOR ME

I constantly have to ask myself how I can run a profitable business and not be sucked into the seductive power of money. How do I also manage our personal finances, so it doesn't become an obsession? I have my own set of safeguards.

The first strategy is a mindset: simply recognizing that money is a dangerous power and not taking it too lightly. When dealing with a dangerous foe, our first objective is to disarm him. As Ellul argues, the most effective way to diminish another's power is to devalue it. If I don't value what the foe stands for, they no longer have the upper hand.

If someone tries to blackmail you because they have secret information about you but if you don't care whether the information is made public, then they have no power over you. If a customer makes unreasonable demands and threatens to take their business elsewhere, if you don't care about losing their business, their threats mean nothing.

The same applies to money. If we simply recognize it as a tool and not our main objective in business, nor our primary motivation to work, we have already taken the first step in disarming it.

The second strategy in disarming the power of money is more than just theory or words. It requires practical application. When we're fortunate enough to be profitable in business, or have a lucrative career, what do we do with the money? As our businesses grow, there are endless needs of upgrading equipment and of hiring and rewarding staff. So knowing what to do with the profit is obvious.

On a personal level, during the child-rearing years, it was

easy to obsess about not having enough. The challenge was never having too much money, but rather how to pay all the bills. School supplies, medical bills, a mortgage, and transportation were constant needs, not to mention food and clothing.

It's when we become more profitable to the point of excess profit, or when the checkbook is suddenly in the black because the kids are grown and out of the house that our hearts, motivations, and wisdom are tested in a different way. How much do we keep for ourselves? Do our lifestyles rise to our level of income?

Not having enough, or having more than we need are two sides of the same coin—worshiping money versus recognizing God as the source of our provision.

Nonessential wealth— do our lifestyles rise to our level of income?

Reflecting back on the study of money and Ellul's contention that it's a power to disarm, my wife and I made a pact before we returned to Wisconsin. No matter how profitable the business may become, we were going to set our lifestyle at a limit. Back then, the number was around $40,000 a year. We viewed it as a spiritual discipline to live within our means.

The choice in the cars we drove, the house we bought, groceries, eating out, recreation, and luxuries all had to fit within our budget. If the business thrived, we shared the profits with our employees; however, that didn't mean we could personally increase our lifestyle. At that time, we determined we would give the excess to charity. It was a rather simplistic attempt to keep money from taking us over, but it worked.

The discipline of dividing our weekly paycheck into mortgage and car payments, insurance bills, and the cash envelopes for groceries, clothing, date night, and emergencies instilled habits that we still live by almost thirty years later. For years, I had the oldest and rustiest vehicle in our company's parking lot, which perplexed some of our employees.

We have never bought a new vehicle during our marriage. My wife still shops at thrift stores, and almost all of our clothes are sale items or purchased with coupons. As our family expanded, we needed to raise the level of income we allowed ourselves to consume. However, we still forced ourselves to live within a new budget. Vacations were researched for deals and off-peak times. Even though we love to ski as a family, we sought out smaller, less expensive resorts, and usually had to save for two years to be able to afford a trip. Credit cards always had to be paid off in full each month. Top priority was always given to paying off our mortgage debt.

Financial advisors tell us we exercised wise financial discipline. It's simply good money sense to live within our means and not pay interest on loans, something our government has difficulty grasping. My parents modeled this for me out of necessity.

However, as the business flourished, there was a constant temptation to buy more, spend more, have a little nicer car, take a little nicer vacation, and simply enjoy the fruits of our labors. What's wrong with that? As it is with my struggles with addiction, it's playing with fire, and I needed boundaries and limits.

As we have gotten older, this issue has become even more complex, as our financial discipline has yielded much fruit. As we kept investing back into the company, our state-of-the-art equipment yielded more profit. As we were able to raise wages and benefits to attract and keep top talent, the business yielded more profit. As the business became more profitable, we had a difficult time giving so much away.

As we partnered with charities, we discovered that our large donations sometimes created unhealthy dependencies and/or mismanagement of our donations. We continually wrestle with the question about how much we should give to our employees, reinvest back into the company, and give to charity. Although we may take steps to disarm money in our personal lives, if we give away large amounts to others, are we contributing to their corruption?

Over the years, our view on philanthropy, business investment, and being good stewards of money has continued to evolve. I'll explore this a bit more in a later chapter, but the point is, we have to recognize that the power that money holds needs to be disarmed. This is an underlying principle that guides almost all financial decisions—from how we quote jobs to compensation for our employees to reinvesting back into the company.

It also lays the simple foundation for how we do business, which we'll now explore in more detail.

5

Is the Golden Rule Good for Business?

His message sounded eerily familiar. I sat in his office, seeking advice on how to manage our growth, as well as sharing my personal despair in being overwhelmed.

His advice was simple but counterintuitive. "If you don't grow, you will personally die." He meant I needed to grow the company so I could afford to hire more staff, to take some load off myself. I initially hated to hear this, as I thought more employees meant more problems and stress.

Years later, I had to admit he was right. In this case, bigger was better. As we grew, we were able to distribute the work to more staff, which provided more meaningful employment for more families, which meant serving more customers in our industry. But unlike that angry customer who wanted to grow just for the money, we were growing to be more influential in our corner of the world.

Seeking God's kingdom and His righteousness gives plenty of opportunities in business for practical application of true inner goodness. When dealing with customers, what is often referred to as the Golden Rule is not just common sense but good business sense as well.

> **Golden Rule in the workplace: Do to others what you'd have them do to you.**

The Golden Rule is established in Matthew 7:12, where Jesus says, "So in everything, do to others what you would have them do to you." In the business context, treat your customers and vendors as you'd want to be treated.

This seems to be common sense, and yet, when the pressure's on to pay your bills, the temptation is always there to make a killing, so to speak, if the opportunity arises.

For example, in our business, customers often look to us when their equipment is broken to get them up and running as soon as possible. We've had numerous situations over the years when entire factories had to shut down because of one broken gear. Modern printing presses can fill a building the size of a football field and employ hundreds of people. If just one critical gear breaks, the entire press may have to be shut down and everyone sent home.

We once had a meat processing plant that was waiting to butcher ten thousand turkeys, but a critical sprocket broke, and the slaughtering had to be put on hold. The life of the turkeys had to be extended until we could get our customer a new sprocket. This might sound amusing, but feeding and watering ten thousand turkeys is no simple, or inexpensive, task.

When these rush jobs happen, our customers don't care about the price nearly as much as how quickly they can get a new gear or sprocket. Time is of the essence, and they will pay almost any price to save even a few hours. In these cases, we need to charge an expedite fee, since the work disturbs our production schedules, requires us to work overtime (sometimes through the night), and may require pulling off numerous other jobs and setting up just for their gear.

Since additional costs are incurred, the customer always expects to pay for the expedited delivery. This is an opportunity to make a huge profit. From a business standpoint, shouldn't we make as much profit as possible? We could argue the benefits of giving the employees bonuses, paying down debt, being able to purchase new equipment, as well as pocketing a little extra cash for ourselves. If our business existed primarily to make money, there would be no such concept as being greedy, and we would charge as much as possible. This is exactly how one of our competitors operates. For years, they openly advertised different price structures on their website based on how quickly the customer needed a gear.

Normally, it would take them three or more weeks to make a custom gear. If the gear was needed in two weeks, they would charge 50 percent more. If it was needed in a week, they would charge 200 percent more. The costs increased to the point that a customer would have to pay as much as 2,000 percent more if it was needed in 24 hours.

One of our customers once asked us to quote on a simple set

of gears they needed in a few days. When I gave them the price, they called back to ask if we misquoted the job. I responded that I didn't think so, but that I'd review it. I called them back and told them the price we gave them was accurate. They then proceeded to tell me what the aforementioned competition wanted to charge. It was more than ten times our price.

No matter how you analyzed it, there wasn't any justification for their outrageous price except to maximize their profit at the customer's expense. They were simply taking advantage of the customer's misfortune. In my opinion, exhibiting true inner goodness doesn't allow for such business practices.

EXCESSIVE TRUE INNER GOODNESS

Early on, Jesus lays aside the perception that being truly good is merely a religious matter only for Sundays. God's goodness, His righteousness, is not something we simply hear about in a sermon and intellectually agree with. It's a force to be reckoned with that stands in direct opposition to the dung we face every day in our work worlds. God's goodness doesn't tolerate the corruption, slander, gossip, jealousy, laziness, greed, cheating, stealing, lying, or hating all around us. His goodness is not a noun but a verb, a conviction that is born in our hearts and acted out in the form of our day-to-day decisions.

Consider when Jesus addresses His disciples and the crowds who came to hear Him teach. "You are the salt of the earth. But if the salt loses its saltiness, how can it be made salty again? It's no longer good for anything, except to be thrown out and trampled underfoot" (Matt. 5:13).

In our modern world of refrigerators and freezers, we lose

some of the impact of Jesus saying we're the "salt of the earth." He's not just talking about table salt to flavor our food. Talking to fishermen in a desert climate, He knew most people understood the vital role salt played as a preservative. Fish and other meats needed to be heavily salted to arrest decay and keep the meat from spoiling. If the salt was not salty enough, it was useless and thrown out.

Like salt, God's goodness impedes the rot and spoilage in our world. So if we, His vessels of His true inner goodness, don't reflect God's goodness in all our daily transactions, we're quite worthless in terms of representing God's kingdom.

Jesus continues, "You are the light of the world. A town built on a hill cannot be hidden. Neither do people light a lamp and put it under a bowl. Instead they put it on its stand, and it gives light to everyone in the house. In the same way, let your light shine before others, that they may see your good deeds and glorify your Father in heaven" (Matt. 5:14–16).

The world is often a dark place in desperate need of hope, peace, love, truth, kindness, gentleness, forgiveness, encouragement, generosity, fairness, meaning, and purpose. We see it in the eyes and hearts of our students, employees, and customers. Does anybody care? Is there any sense of a greater purpose and meaning to life? Are we simply cogs in a huge machine, where our jobs are just a place to earn a paycheck so we can buy stuff that will hopefully make us feel better?

Or is there a grand design and plan, where our gifts and talents find expression, where we have a sense we're needed and have a vital role to play?

As followers of Jesus, our lives should exude meaning, purpose, goodness, and a commitment to excellence on every level.

Like lighthouses in pitch darkness, our good deeds illuminate the ideal potential and possibilities of our human existence. If our businesses are an extension of our personal goodness, they can be salt, light, and a city on a hill, measured by our conduct in day-to-day affairs.

Returning to our topic of making a profit, our true inner goodness determines how much we charge for our products.

What does true inner goodness look like in business?

For example, when we quote jobs, we need to be vigilant in charging enough to make a fair profit without charging so much that we take advantage of the customer. Like many custom manufacturers, we operate from calculated shop rates, meaning we figure how much each operation of making a gear costs to be able to pay for the machine tools, the wages, and the overhead expenses. After a job is complete, we do a cost analysis of the job that compares our quoted cost to what the actual costs were.

For example, in overly simplistic terms, if we estimated that a particular gear would take five hours to manufacture, and each operation's rate is $50 per hour, we would quote the customer $250. After the gear is complete, our cost analysis shows the true cost. If it took six hours, the true cost was $300 and we made $50 less than was needed to make a necessary profit. If it took four hours, the true cost is $200, we made $50 more than it took to make a profit.

Quoting jobs is really an educated guess, based on our experience. So as long as our true cost is somewhat close to our quoted cost, we're pleased and confident the customer got a fair price.

But what happens when we grossly underestimate or overestimate the cost of the gear? If we were too low in our estimated price, not only did we fail to make a profit, we didn't even make enough money to cover our expenses of materials, wages, and overhead. Obviously, we wouldn't stay in business very long if we did this very often.

On the other hand, if we were too high on our estimated cost, our profit may be huge, but did we give the customer a fair price? Of course, the argument could be made that we're worth the high cost because our expertise is worth the huge profit and the customer is happy with the price—so what's the problem?

The Golden Rule suggests what the problem is: Are we doing to our customers what we would want done to us? If we were our customer needing a gear, would we want to be charged a high price just because Edgerton Gear is the only gear shop in town?

"Of course not," we answer, because we all want to be treated justly. However, the next argument is, Who is to say what is fair or just? Edgerton Gear has spent five decades gaining wisdom, knowledge, expertise, and equipment to make a quality gear at a reasonable price, so isn't it okay if we make a huge profit once in a while?

I could agree with this argument; however, there is a quiet voice that goes off in my head that says it's wrong. *Treat the customer as I want to be treated.* Besides, if we're intent on disarming the power of money, which is a spiritual battle we face every day, we need to refuse to give in to the temptation of excessive profit. This is a practical example of radical obedience to the kingdom of God and true inner goodness.

Remember John the Baptist, who was the forerunner of Jesus? His vision of God's coming kingdom struck a nerve with the religious elites but awakened the hearts of the common man and woman. They asked Him what they should do to be part of this radical new reality. He instructed them to be generous. "Anyone who has two shirts should share with the one who has none, and anyone who has food should do the same" (Luke 3:11). When it came to the lowly tax collectors, his response should hit every business person in the gut: "Don't collect any more than you are required to" (v.13).

So, what actually happens when our price is too high or too low?

If we're too low, we do some research to determine why. Did we simply miscalculate the cost? Did we miss something on the blueprint that required additional operations and costs? Or did our machinists run into unexpected problems, such as a machine malfunction? Or did they simply have a bad day?

If we believe we could do better next time, we simply absorb the loss and chalk it up to experience. But if we know we really do need to charge more for future orders, we contact the customer, honestly explain our dilemma, and inform them that if they order the same gear in the future, the cost will be higher.

I empathize with business owners in extremely competitive markets, where profit margins are razor thin. You worry about paying your bills and your staff, and you may have to forgo paying yourself. In these cases, the marketplace can be brutally harsh. Sometimes your business may not survive, due to a number of factors, such as competition, an increase in operating costs, or obsolescence. However, there are also times a customer is willing to pay more because you're valuable to them and they trust you to be fair.

If our profit's determined to be too high, we again do our research. If it's determined that we can consistently make the gear or gears for considerably less than what we charged, we will often contact the customer *before* we invoice them and explain why we need to charge less.

How many phone calls have you received like this? The response we get is usually shock, because the answer tends to be zero. With one of our larger customers, they often give us projects that are very extensive, with multiple parts made out of stainless steel. These are very difficult to manufacture, with many potential problems in every operation. We quote these jobs using a worst-case scenario, but if the job goes smoothly, we gladly notify the customer about how much less their bill will be. It's joyful for them (and us) when, at the completion of the job, we can notify them about the reduced price.

Several times we've been able to reduce our price by as much as 10 percent, which might represent thousands of dollars. Some folks argue this is absurd and we're fools for not taking as much money as the customer agreed to pay. However, I argue this always results in a new level of trust and appreciation from our customers. It's wise never to forget that our success is tied to our customers' success. Rarely will they go anywhere else for their gears.

True inner goodness builds customer loyalty, but it's much more than a good business strategy. Treating others as we would want to be treated is simply the right thing to do from a kingdom perspective.

BEYOND THE GOLDEN RULE

Jesus has a way of drawing us in, setting us up, and then blowing apart our current worldview. We started this chapter with the

Golden Rule in Matthew 7:12, treating others as we wish to be treated. However, notice what He says later in chapter 22 when the religious elite are unhappy with His teaching and are trying to trick Him into giving a politically *incorrect* answer. They asked Him His opinion on the greatest commandment from God.

> Jesus replied: "'Love the Lord your God with all your heart and with all your soul and with all your mind.' This is the first and greatest commandment. And the second is like it: 'Love your neighbor as yourself.' All the Law and the Prophets hang on these two commandments." (Matt. 22:37–39)

Many of us who have attended church at some point in our lives have heard that we're to love God with all our heart, soul, and mind. Jesus is quoting the Old Testament book of Deuteronomy (6:5). In their culture, this was an especially important teaching that everyone knew. Having only one God was their religious distinctive.

Who is my "neighbor" in the workplace?

We've probably also heard we're to love our neighbors as ourselves. This is what good neighbors do; we watch out for each other.

But if we're honest, we often have neighbors who aren't like us—maybe they're a little wacky or downright unlikable. How many of us as kids growing up had a neighbor who had a reputation (deserved or not) for being crazy, mean, or dangerous? Yet we may have gone to Sunday school and been told to love them.

My usual argument was that the Bible didn't say we had to

like them, just love them, which I justified as just being careful not to get on their bad side. So when I grew up and worked in the family business, it occurred to me that my "neighbors" included our customers and vendors. I used the same logic. I didn't have to like them, but I was supposed to love them. So don't tick them off—it's bad for business.

> **Loving my neighbor *is* *like* loving God.**

However, Jesus used just six words when He linked the greatest commandment and the second greatest commandment.

"'Love the Lord your God with all your heart and with all your soul and with all your mind.' This is the first and greatest commandment. And the second is like it: 'Love your neighbor as yourself.'"

And the second is like it. Loving your neighbor is like loving God. Therefore, not loving my neighbor is like not loving God. Ouch. If I claim any allegiance to God at all, how I treat my customers, vendors, and employees is related to how I treat God. Would I dare rip God off, charge Him too much? Would I treat God poorly, be overly demanding, and not pay a fair wage?

Luke has a similar and more in-depth description of Jesus' encounter with the teachers of the Law who were trying to trap Him. One of them stands up and asks Jesus what he must do to inherit eternal life. Jesus responds this time with questions. "What is written in the Law? How do you read it?" The teacher responds by quoting those same two directives.

Jesus basically tells him that he gave the correct answer, and should go and do it (Luke 10:28). However, the teacher can't leave well enough alone, and he asks Jesus to define the word "neighbor." Jesus answers with the parable of the Good Samaritan.

THE TRUE INNER GOODNESS SAMARITAN

Most people in our society, even if they've never been to church, have come across this familiar story at some point. Found in Luke 10, it's about a man traveling from Jerusalem to Jericho, a dangerous road. He's attacked, stripped, robbed, beaten, and left for dead.

A priest comes along, sees the victim, and avoids him. A Levite (a religious man) does the same. But a Samaritan comes along, sees the traveler's plight, and is emotionally moved. He bandages the man's wounds, hoists him to his donkey, and carries him to an inn, where he can heal. He also leaves instructions to forward any medical expenses to him, the Samaritan.

As Jesus finishes the story, his questioner is forced to admit that the third man, the kind one, was the victim's neighbor. Jesus says, "Go and do likewise" (v. 37).

It's difficult for readers today to appreciate how offensive this story was to the supposed experts in the Law who were questioning Jesus. The Jewish elite didn't appreciate Jesus' point that a lowly Samaritan could somehow qualify as a neighbor. As Jack Wellman explains, Samaritans were a despised people, considered half-breeds (Jewish and Gentile). There had been intermarriage when the old Judean kingdom had broken down, and these people had settled in the land called Samaria, just north.

When the Jews had returned from captivity in another country, they'd tried to rebuild their temple—only to receive resistance from the Samaritans, who'd pour blood from pigs on the ground to make the area unclean. Jews would walk far out of their way to avoid impurifying themselves by occupying Samaritan ground.[1]

Jesus placed the Samaritan in the good-guy role for a reason. He knew it was offensive, and that underlined His point: true inner goodness is about what we do, not who it's for.

I grew up surrounded by racism. If you weren't white, you were automatically a target. But you had to be *really* white, as in European white, like Swedish, Norwegian, German, Polish, or English white. If there was any color to your skin, as in Italian or Greek, you were a target. The darker your skin, the more vile and disgusting the slander—the one exception being Asian.

There was a different class of hatred for Asians, supposedly left over from World War II and the Korean War. The racist jokes from my relatives and friends were constant. Maybe it's human nature to fear and hate those whom we don't understand.

From the 1960s and 70s, I don't recall ever knowing a classmate of color from kindergarten all the way to twelfth grade—so that when a few African and Latino Americans moved into our town, I seriously feared for their lives. Hatred of any other ethnic group ran deep in my family and in my dad's social circles.

When I moved to California, I was both afraid of and amazed at the diversity. When I attended college, I took every class I could on minority studies, as I was hungry to understand their cultures. I eventually became close friends with many different people of color over the years, and have come to appreciate our differences and struggles.

Ironically, much of this appreciation actually came from my father, who was one of the most racist men I've ever known. However, my dad was a paradox. In his private life, he'd join in with the racist jokes to a degree that embarrassed me. Although he did have fond memories of a fellow soldier in the army who was black, all other ethnicities were severely ridiculed.

Yet whenever anyone came to our shop in need of a gear, my dad always treated them with respect and dignity, with the exception of anyone who was belligerent or rude. It didn't matter what color or class they were; he treated them as a valuable customer. It could be argued that he did this because it was good business sense, but I'm convinced there was something deeper going on in my dad than just a desire to make a buck.

I remember numerous times when Dad would charge little or nothing when a walk-in customer had an emergency. It confused me when he'd join in the most disgusting, racist jokes about black people, then treat Moses, a black machine repairman from Chicago, as if he were royalty. Most of the time when Moses visited, it was an emergency, because his customers were broken down. He couldn't get the service he needed from any other gear shop in Chicago, so he'd drive the two to three hours north to see my father.

Dad would always help him out, sometimes working late into the night. When I took over the shop years later, I had the privilege of working with Moses myself. He was big, intimidating, and very direct. He took his job seriously, and time was of the essence to get his customer up and running again. It was clear he thought I couldn't live up to my dad's reputation of meeting his needs. He made it *very* clear to me that my dad set the bar very high, and I had better make sure I made it worth his time to drive so far.

I didn't disappoint Moses, and I even came to enjoy his visits. He always spoke very highly of my father, pointing out how my dad would go out of his way to help him and sometimes not charge as much as he should have. Dad treated everyone like this. So how could my dad seemingly hate black people, yet humbly treat them with respect and dignity when they showed up at the shop?

Reflecting on this, I think it's easy yet cowardly to be a bar-stool racist, bellying up to the bar, having a few drinks, and laughing with your buddies, telling raunchy racist jokes. But when our prejudices have a name and a face, when we see in their eyes that their humanity and struggles are just like our struggles, and when there is no one to laugh at our jokes, it's much more difficult to be filled with hate.

Who is my neighbor in Edgerton Gear? From a kingdom perspective, I'm challenged to answer that it's anyone who walks in the door in need of mercy. This can be very challenging at times and requires strong doses of wisdom and discernment. Is the customer really in need or are they just looking to take advantage of our good will, as in the hatchet man story in the opening chapter?

If the customer is truly in need of help, are we the ones to provide it? Sometimes, our equipment and skill set aren't the best fit for the customer, and they're best served by directing them to another shop. Usually, however, they came to us because we're the best ones to help, but their timing may be very inconvenient, as on a Friday afternoon or right before the Christmas holiday. I've often wondered over the years if God doesn't sometimes probe our willingness to serve and love Him by sending us needy customers at the worst possible times.

Here's another thought: Are we actually held accountable for *not* extending kindness, when it was in our power to do so? Am I actually supposed to love *everyone*, even the rude customer, the shoddy vendor, and the kid off the street asking for a job who shows up in cut-off jeans pulled halfway down his rear, a hoody covering his face, and an attitude that says we should be thankful he's applying at our place of business?

At this point, the cynical and skeptical side of me rears its ugly head and screams that this kind of thinking is impossibly impractical. How many times over the years have I loathed dealing with certain customers or vendors? What about employees who betrayed us, stole from us, and slandered our name and reputation? What about all the times I'm exhausted, stressed, and in an incredibly foul mood? Does God really expect me to be loving all the time?

The business world isn't like going to a church building once a week, dressing up and smiling to everyone even though we fought in the car all the way there. Anyone can put on a good face for an hour or so, but having to work with people forty to sixty hours per week means everyone gets to see the good, bad, and ugly in each other and in ourselves. What does love look like then?

I sometimes wonder whether God is looking down at me with a scowl and challenging me, "Come on, smart guy, answer me! Can you really say you've always been loving to everyone who walks through your door, sends you an email, or calls you on the phone?"

Regrettably, the clear answer is no. In fact, anger, bitterness, cynicism, and stress come out of me more than I care to admit. Fortunately, loving others isn't dependent on my mood, nor does God judge me based on my ability or inability to love others.

Does God judge me at all? Is He like the old schoolteacher standing over us with a ruler, ready to smack me the moment I step out of line? Or is He more like a mix between Mr. Miyagi from the movie *Karate Kid*[2] and Mother Teresa: wise, patient, disciplined yet encouraging, always cheering me on, seeing beyond what I think are my limits to what He sees as possible?

When He says to seek His righteousness, am I to muster up some goodness in me that may or may not exist? Or does He really mean He wants to allow His true inner goodness to fill my true emptiness?

Not my true inner goodness but God's goodness in me and through me.

If Jesus is who He says He is, and if God is who Jesus says He is, then my job isn't to be the perfect Christian business person or leader, but to simply be a person through whom God can work.

In the worst of times over the years, as I've struggled with my addictions, anger, and exhaustion, I always fall back on Jesus' response to a simple question, put to Him by the crowds after He famously fed five thousand of them with just a few loaves of bread and a handful of fish. Predictably, that miracle got their attention, and, as with today's cult worship of celebrities, people wanted more of Him.

Realizing they wanted to force Him to be their king, Jesus gave everyone, disciples included, the slip. He withdrew by Himself into the mountains.

I wonder whether even His disciples were a bit perplexed by His need to be alone, because when evening fell, they jumped into the boat and headed across the lake. That set the stage for the famous story of Jesus freaking them out by walking on water and quieting the storm.

The next day, the crowds, realizing that Jesus somehow

ditched them, went in search of Him and discovered Him on the other side of the lake. Questioned on how He got there, Jesus answered as follows, knowing their motives for finding Him.

> "You've come looking for me not because you saw God in my actions but because I fed you, filled your stomachs—and for free. Don't waste your energy striving for perishable food like that. Work for the food that sticks with you, food that nourishes your lasting life, food the Son of Man provides. He and what he does are guaranteed by God the Father to last." (John 6:26–27 MSG)

I'm confident this reply was a bit confusing, since they were probably still thinking of the tasty fish and chips from the day before. Was that the kind of food that sticks with you? Food that nourishes our lasting life? If it's anything like the day before, why not? Who wouldn't want to cut down on their grocery bill?

The people asked Him to clarify what God wanted them to do. Jesus replied, "The work of God is this: to believe in the one he has sent" (John 6:29).

I'm not going to speculate whether these people had even a clue about what He was talking about, as the story was still unfolding. He hadn't been crucified yet, or raised from the dead. There were no New Testament theologians around to break the lesson into handy bullet points.

However, we have the luxury of hindsight; we understand Jesus was talking about faith. It's not a mere intellectual faith, as in believing something is true, like an answer to an algebra problem. The word *believe* carried much more weight and was connected to action, such as "I believe I'll be and feel healthier if

I get some exercise, so therefore I'll exercise."

Simply agreeing that exercise is good for you wouldn't do much good if you continue sitting on your couch, eating pizza and cheese balls. *Believe* in this context was more in line with reorienting how we live our life to be in line with how God intended.

Eugene Peterson's translation of verse 29 hits the mark: "Throw your lot in with the One that God has sent. That kind of a commitment gets you in on God's works" (John 6:29 MSG).

So consider our dilemma of loving our neighbor and our inability to exhibit true inner goodness toward everyone who crosses our path and in every situation we face in business. God doesn't demand we get it right every time. Rather, He wants us to open ourselves up to Him so He can work in and through us. As our actions are guided by "throwing in our lot" with Jesus and His way of dealing with life, we begin to discover that our businesses, which are extensions of ourselves, can be a transforming force in a culture that is in desperate need of some out-of-this-world yet still-in-this-world goodness.

6

Relational Transactions

The inspector was wrong. The engineers were wrong. The purchasing agent was wrong.

The gears were almost perfect. I say "almost" because there is no such thing as a perfect gear. But these were pretty darn close.

They far exceeded the quality the customer required and requested, yet they couldn't understand, recognize, or appreciate the simple fact that they were wrong and we were right.

As some of our machinists say, "you can't fix stupid." But it wouldn't go over very well if I told our customer they all were being stupid. Somehow, I had to figure out how to overcome their ignorance and arrogance. Their success depended on it and, because they were one of our very substantial customers, ours did, too.

We have a saying in our shop: "Making gears is easy. It's people that are difficult." Although our equipment occasionally breaks down and needs maintenance, our lathes, mills, and hobbers (a type of milling machine that cuts gear teeth) are never moody, always show up, are fairly predictable, and don't get easily offended or defensive. We don't have to figure out whether the machines will get along with each other or enjoy their work.

People, on the other hand, are in another dimension of challenge and complexity. I often feel like my day is one big minefield of navigating people and their moods, while being aware of my own anxiety and stress. I often hear that we are supposed to leave our personal lives at home and not bring them into work.

> **Successful Business = A Sum of Successful Relational Transactions.**

This is impossible. We're all human, with our own unique set of joys, sorrows, defeats, and triumphs. None of us are capable of leaving it all at the door.

Business, at its most basic level, is a series of relational transactions. I may have to deal with a disgruntled or struggling coworker. Or I may be struggling and I don't want to project my stress onto others. We may not have met a customer's expectations, and they're ticked off. A vendor may have screwed up and may or may not want guidance on how to fix the problem.

My day gets overwhelmingly stressful when I have too many relational transactions. Too often, this is when I make poor decisions, offend someone, or fail to serve the other person as I should. I've come to understand that business = the sum of relational transactions. Therefore, successful business = the sum of all successful relational transactions. So, my challenge is how to be certain that at least the majority of my relational transactions are successful.

The world's goal of doing business is to make money. To make money, we need to make sales. To make sales, we must have an attractive product that meets a customer's needs or wants, and persuade them to give us their money for our product. For most businesses in the world, building a relationship with the customer is only a means to an end: to make a sale.

> **For a kingdom company, the relational aspect of the business transaction is just as important as making a sale.**

However, for a kingdom company, the relational aspect of the business transaction is just as important as making a sale. If we consider the two greatest commandments of loving God and neighbor, and we learned that our neighbor includes everyone we work with, such as customers, vendors, and coworkers, and we're called to treat this neighbor as we want to be treated—then it follows that every aspect of running our business becomes a relational transaction. From product development, to advertising, to manufacturing, recruiting, hiring, training, sales, shipping, and invoicing—it's all relational transactions.

We make gears for all sorts of equipment all over the world. It's sometimes difficult to think of making gears as a relational transaction. We take a piece of steel, put it through two or more machine operations, and *voila!* we have a gear. But without relationships, we would not only be unaware that our customer needs a gear, but we wouldn't be able to obtain the steel, machines, tooling, and the machinists to make the gear. Every step of the process requires human interactions. If there is a breakdown in any of these relational interactions, the entire process fails.

So, what makes a relational transaction successful? To answer this question, try to guess how many relational transactions you're part of every day. Is it twenty? Perhaps fifty?

Seriously, think about this for a minute. From the moment you open your eyes in the morning until you fall asleep at night, how many times have you interacted with someone? This would include not only up-close-and-personal interactions, but also emails, phone calls, and anything electronic.

If we break down relational transactions to the most basic level, my guess is your average day has hundreds if not thousands of relational transactions, and you judge your day solely on whether the majority of them were either successful or not. Think I'm stretching it a bit?

Consider this: If you're in any form of leadership, such as a parent, teacher, manager, team leader, clerk at a convenience store, phone receptionist, or business owner, you have the power to influence someone else's life. Think about the very first moment you encounter another human being on any given day. Are you or they the first to say good morning, or is it said at all?

If the other person says it first with a perky smile, how does that make you feel, versus if they grunt at you with a sour demeanor?

If you frequent a coffee shop on the way to work, is the barista glad to see you, or does he or she convey a contempt for the job, for you, for the day? What does that do to your mood?

Think of your coworkers or fellow commuters. What does it feel like if they're angry, impatient, and in a bad mood? Do you work in a company or have you been to a place of business that just has a foul, dark feel, where nobody smiles? Or have you ever really enjoyed working with someone or been to a business where almost everyone seemed happy, engaged, and glad to be there?

Whether we realize it or not, our days are filled with hundreds of moments where we're either positively or negatively affecting someone else's well-being. Still don't believe me? Consider the following.

Tom Shadyac is one of Hollywood's most famous directors of comedies. His movies have grossed over $2 billion at the box office. Some of the silly movies you might know are *Ace Ventura: Pet Detective*, *Bruce Almighty*, and *Liar Liar*. After a near death experience, Shadyac went on a quest to discover the meaning of life and told his story in a documentary titled *I AM*.[1] It's a fascinating quest, as he explores what makes people happy and seeks out the world's renowned psychologists, philosophers, and religious leaders.

One of the strangest but most compelling parts of the movie is when he goes to the Heart Math Institute and meets a scientist named Rollin McCraty. McCraty shows Shadyac that our moods and thoughts have a profound effect on the electrical energy field that emanates from our bodies. Now, before you label me a New Ager and angrily toss this book into the trash or fireplace, the fact remains that our bodies are one big bundle of energy. Science can't completely explain what causes us to be alive but can actually measure our electrical impulses. In the documentary, McCraty hooks up electrodes to a dish of yogurt with an amp meter. He sets the dish in front of Shadyac and asks him to think of unpleasant thoughts. Shadyac is not touching the yogurt. Believe it or not, the live yogurt cultures are sensitive to Shadyac's negative thoughts and mood and actually react enough to be measured electronically.

I'm not a scientist, so I can't vouch for any of this. Maybe it's all a bunch of malarkey, but intuitively, this makes sense to me. What we often don't realize, or acknowledge, is how interconnected we are. Being around someone who is in a bad mood undoubtedly affects us in ways we often don't understand or can't explain. My staff has told me they can feel when I'm stressed out or in a bad mood, no matter how hard I try to hide it. They say my mood can change and/or set the entire mood of the office.

Are we having a positive or negative effect on the person or persons with whom we're interacting?

Like it or not, we all affect each other, so when I talk about relational transactions, the question is, "Is the transaction successful or unsuccessful?" In other words, are we having a positive or negative effect on the person or persons with whom we're interacting?

We usually have more interactions with those we work with than with those we don't work with. It's where we spend the majority of our lives, and, by nature, business is about transactions. Our day is a constant stream of give and take. It's a series of transactions, where both parties are attempting to get what they want and/or need.

When a customer calls, they want something. Do we meet their need, and do they, in turn, meet our need to be compensated in some form for our service to them? When a coworker asks for help, do we meet their need and help them with a friendly attitude, or do we make them feel they're intruding and bothering us?

When someone says "Good morning" to us, basically they're acknowledging us and want or need to be acknowledged in return as a valuable human being. Do we meet this need or dismiss them, communicating we don't value them at all?

When the clerk at the gas station says thank you, longing to be appreciated in his or her service job, do we take them for granted and ignore it, or do we thank this person in return, acknowledging service we've received?

Does the culture of our company exude a desire to serve others, an appreciation for them, and a sincere motive to meet their needs?

I could go on and on, but the point is simply that every transaction we have with anyone throughout our day is an opportunity for either a successful or unsuccessful relational transaction.

In business, it's paramount to get this reality into our heads. Does the culture of our company exude a desire to serve others, an appreciation for them, and a sincere motive to meet their needs? You may have an amazing product, with an amazing talent pool, and an untapped market with a huge need. But if there is a breakdown in any of the relational transactions throughout the entire process of developing, manufacturing, marketing, growing a supplier base, banking, hiring, shipping, invoicing, collecting, and investing, then the entire venture is affected.

A spirit of service must be part of your DNA. It starts with you as a leader and must penetrate into the feelings and experiences of your staff. If it doesn't exist inside you, you can't expect it on the outside, where you interact with your staff, customers, and vendors. Even the internal metrics that are usually used to measure financial health are, in actuality, measuring the relational health of minute-by-minute transactions.

If you think of success as a sum of successful relational transactions, then processes and metrics are simply the tools to keep you focused and accountable to the larger goals.

For example, in our business, in the process of making a gear, we use in-process inspection reports. Every operation requires a machinist to document the print specifications and tolerances and the actual measurements of their work to ensure the gear is made to the customer's specifications. The machinist is then required to have another machinist check their work by reinspecting and documenting their findings.

It's not that we don't trust the actual machinist to do his or her job; we're more concerned about the bigger goal of serving our customer. We're human and make mistakes, so our process of the inspection reports and the relational transaction of having the machinists hold each other accountable to high quality standards assures that our customer gets the product they need.

This level of accountability builds trust between our customers and us, which usually leads to a lasting business relationship. If one of the machinists is in a bad mood, disrespectful of others, and makes her coworkers feel uncomfortable or hesitant to check the other's work, the end result is potentially that bad parts reach the customer. The relationship with the customer suffers, and our entire business is affected.

With every single business I know, without exception—whether it's a small mom-and-pop café or a huge multinational corporation—that company's biggest strength or biggest weakness is the relational health of the day-to-day transactions that comprise their business. What is the quality of the relationships among the staff, with their customers, and with their vendors? Does everyone feel valued, respected, and appreciated? Or are there varying levels of bitterness, jealousy, apathy, selfishness, and disrespect?

As consumers, we intuitively know whether there are problems with a company, because we ultimately feel the effects. The product may not be delivered on time, it may be of poor quality, or perhaps the buying experience simply wasn't pleasant. If we were privy to peeking into the company and

> **Our biggest strength or biggest weakness is the relational health of the day-to-day transactions that comprise our business.**

looking under the hood, the culprit would most likely be poor relational health.

Maybe the boss is a hard-driving knucklehead who abuses his staff, or maybe coworkers refuse to get along. Maybe the company has a reputation of beating up on their suppliers for better pricing, to the point that suppliers are resentful as their profit margins become razor thin. Maybe it's simply a poor management structure, where too few are doing too much and the work load isn't shared equitably. There could be and often are a thousand reasons for relational breakdowns. The challenge is to address them and establish a foundation of relational health.

One of my favorite passages in the gospels is when two of Jesus' disciples are plotting their advancement up the corporate ladder, so to speak, at the expense of their teammates. The two brothers, James and John, ask Jesus for a favor. They want Him to make arrangements to be His right-hand and left-hand men "in glory," when He comes into His kingdom.

Jesus is disappointed in them. He asks them, in so many

words, if they think they can handle the "baptism" He's about to face.

They tell Him they can't see why not.

Jesus then tells that, actually, they'll face just what He's going to face; that kind of baptism is in their future. But it's not for Him, Jesus, to assign pecking order.

James and John probably figure at least it was worth a try. But when the other disciples catch wind of this conversation, they blow their stacks. Jesus has to pull everybody together and clear the air. This is when He gives them this lesson:

> "You've observed how godless rulers throw their weight around," he said, "and when people get a little power how quickly it goes to their heads. It's not going to be that way with you. Whoever wants to be great must become a servant. Whoever wants to be first among you must be your slave. That is what the Son of Man has done: He came to serve, not to be served—and then to give away his life in exchange for many who are held hostage." (Mark 10:42–45 MSG)

Now, it's easy to judge James and John for being selfish, but if we're honest, wouldn't we secretly be thinking the same thing if we were in their shoes? We all want to get ahead, to feel valued and honored, to be recognized as someone significant.

Over my years in business, I've seen that it's pretty common for staff to want to advance in leadership. My caution to them is to be careful what they wish for. Being top dog is often not what they think it is. In fact, having lots of responsibility, especially for others, can suck the life out of you. The people you're supposedly leading often judge you unfairly; when things go wrong, you're the one who has to take the hits, no matter whose fault it is; and there are often times you have to mediate between competing issues and agendas.

As Jesus points out, the common way leaders deal with this stress is to throw their weight around and just tell people what to do. The infinitely more difficult yet far more effective way of leading is to humbly offer service to those you're leading.

Jesus said He came to serve, not to be served. Is part of our mission in business (relational transactions) then to serve and seek that which was lost, to restore dignity, honor, justice, and wholeness to a broken world? Is this task not carried out one relational transaction at a time?

I think of a recent instance of ordering a piece of steel from a vendor. Over the years, we've developed a friendship through our business dealings. Todd embodies for me a person who truly seeks to serve, not only at work but also in his personal life as well—raising his children and volunteering for community and church events. He'd be the first to let me know if I would be better off ordering a product from his competitor.

At times, he has struggled with his company's structure, leadership, and choice of software, but he does the best he can in a less-than-ideal work environment.

Recently, Todd lost his mother, who was in her eighties. I asked him over the phone how he was coping and he became very emotional; I just let him talk as he needed to. We ended the conversation by thanking each other for our friendship, as the original reason I called, which was to get a quote, was now secondary.

On numerous levels, this phone call was a series of successful relational transactions. Rooted in mutual humility, we both desired to serve the other, to console each other, and also to meet each other's needs on both a professional level and personal level. This kind of moment is actually very common in our company, since one of our culture's foundational pillars is humility.

SERVICE ≠ ABUSE

Okay, so we're called to go out of our way to serve our customers through successful relational transactions. However, we don't live in nirvana, and we're not a bunch of hippies from the 1960s, where everyone sings "Kumbaya," has flower wreaths in their hair, and hangs peace symbols everywhere. This is the business world, which can be tense, cutthroat, and ruthless at times.

A logical question would be, "Wouldn't people take advantage of our goodness and kindness?"

In other words, won't some customers view us as weak, gullible, and easy to bully? To both questions, the answer is, "Of course!" This is the world we live in. In business, everyone, including me, is always looking out for his or her own best interests. On occasion, I've been guilty of being hard on our vendors when I sensed they were trying to take advantage of us. But I would hope our vendors would also acknowledge that at Edgerton Gear, we're also fair and expect a lot out of ourselves, too.

Trust isn't easily given; it must be earned. Probably like you, I've been burned so many times by shady deals and offers that were too good to be true that my default mode is to not trust anyone in business. Words are cheap and almost everyone is greedy for gain.

In business, however, exhibiting true inner goodness doesn't mean we're gullible and stupid. On the contrary, goodness doesn't ignore badness. It exposes it, shines a light on it, and sets the standard for how God wants business to be done. Serving someone doesn't give them permission to abuse us.

There is a fine line between going the extra mile for a customer and being abused by them.

> **True inner goodness doesn't mean we ignore badness. It exposes it, shines a light on it, and sets the standard for how God wants business to be done.**

Jesus fully recognized how harsh and manipulative the world is. I love the advice He gave His disciples when He sent them out on their own.

"Stay alert. This is hazardous work I'm assigning you. You're going to be like sheep running through a wolf pack, so don't call attention to yourselves. Be as cunning as a snake, inoffensive as a dove" (Matt. 10:16 MSG).

Remember back at the beginning of this book, where I discussed the hatchet man our customer hired to try and force us to lower our prices? We've faced hundreds of situations over the years that required gentleness yet cunning. We've all had to deal with customers who were under tremendous stress or who were simply disrespectful and rude.

We all have difficult customers, customers who are overbearing, demanding, incompetent, and ignorant. There are customers who feel a need to "win," who are arrogant enough to want us to bow down to them, and who think we should feel lucky and blessed that they have stooped low enough to give us their time and money for our products.

Unfortunately, there is still a mindset out there of customers treating their suppliers like indentured servants. The old adage of "the customer is always right" is sometimes a tough pill to swallow, especially when the customer is wrong! These situations require more patience and humility than I can sometimes muster.

But if I come back to the ideal of seeking God's way of doing things (His kingdom) and seeking to exhibit His righteousness (true inner goodness), rather than fighting customers, I find myself trying to help them understand how to make their products better and more economical. They're in need of a successful relational transaction. It doesn't help to get defensive and rude back at them. If anything, it makes matters worse. The situation requires us to swallow our pride, not take their bad mood and accusations personally, and carefully listen.

Many years ago, I learned about a tool from Bowen Systems Theory that has helped me defuse stressful situations. The tool is an idea: Be a Non-Anxious Presence. It's easier said than done, but we always try not to get caught up in the emotion of the moment. Some of my staff is much better at it than I am, but it's a constant goal for me.

That said, there are times a customer crosses the line to abuse. In those cases, it's in everyone's best interest to walk away and let the customer become someone else's problem. I see it as part of their and our journey of learning and growing.

Some customers need to learn the hard way that being a butt-head is, in the long run, neither profitable nor fulfilling. I remember a customer a number of years ago who would yell, swear, and be incredibly offensive and rude to our staff. It seemed the nicer we were to him, the meaner he got. Eventually I was reminded of a situation from when I was in fourth grade confronting a bully on the playground. I was a pipsqueak, but I got tired of being his punching bag.

Just like in the movies, I went on the offensive like a mini raging bull, with flailing arms and a death scream. I landed a lucky punch, and the bully ran off crying. So when my staff told me again how rude this particular customer was, I called him up and let him have it. In a nice (or maybe not so nice) way, I said we were done with him. We were tired of his filthy mouth and rude behavior. He could go find another gear shop.

He was stunned and couldn't apologize fast enough. He said he had no idea he was being so offensive. To this day, we continue to marvel at his effort to be polite and respectful when he calls. He's not always successful, but we admire his effort. Though it didn't feel like it at the time, this was actually an example of a successful relational transaction.

There have also been numerous times when we ended a relationship with customers for the simple reason that we were not a good relational fit. No matter how hard we tried, we weren't able to please them, and they always found something to complain about. My father had another saying: Some people aren't happy unless they're complaining.

When such behavior is embedded in a company's culture, sometimes it's not worth the headaches of keeping their business. In these cases, a successful relational transaction is to end the relationship!

7

The Three-Legged Stool

So how do you get through to someone who refuses to believe the facts?

The company's inspector had a fancy chart from a Coordinate Measuring Machine (CMM) that supposedly "proved" the gears were out of tolerance and not made to print. But the inspector was inspecting the part incorrectly. I tried using reason, physics, geometry, and just plain passion to help him understand his errors. I asked if he had actually tried the gear in their machine to see if it would work, and he said they hadn't because he "knew" it wouldn't work.

In desperation, I humbly begged him at least to try putting it in the machine, and I would gladly pay for their time in doing so if the gears didn't work. Tens of thousands of dollars were at stake for both our companies. They needed to deliver their machine to their customer; we needed them to know we were a competent vendor.

Reluctantly, they agreed to my proposal and tried putting the

gears in their machine. Surprise, surprise! The gears worked perfectly.
Another crisis averted, but I kept wondering why trying to serve our customers had to be this difficult.

Let's pretend for the sake of illustration that you're completely blown away by the concept that running your own business can be one of the most effective ways of changing the world imaginable. You're a person who has come to recognize you're not on this planet by accident, and there actually is a Higher Power than yourself, a spiritual being who intimately cares for our world and you personally.

You feel a debt of gratitude to this Higher Power and want your life to matter, to make a difference, and not to be lived selfishly. You discovered you have unique gifts and talents, and you have come up with a product or service that you believe can make the world (or at least a small part of it) a better place. You hope you can make enough money with this service or product to allow you to purchase the necessities of life, such as food, shelter, and clothing.

You even think your product or service has the potential to allow you to purchase more than just the bare necessities, and you can have even more of an impact by providing meaningful employment for others.

You do your research, and you're convinced there is a need (a market) for your product, but you're not sure where to begin. You read everything you can find about starting a business. You study topics such as product development, supply chain management, marketing, accounting, organizational behavior, and best practices for human resources. You consult lawyers, bankers, accountants, insurance agents, payroll, and human resources experts, and you discover that starting a business is more complicated and overwhelming than you imagined. So, you give up and keep your job working for someone else, and that's perfectly fine with you.

However, the company you work for doesn't share your desire to make the world a better place or recognize your gifts and talents. You feel stifled and try to fulfill your feelings of gratitude toward your Higher Power by getting more involved in a local church or congregation. You've been taught that this is where "ministry" happens, where lives are truly changed and where spiritual needs are supposedly met.

But something inside you keeps longing for more, to be outside of the church walls and to live with a sense of purpose and mission that encompasses all your gifts and talents, while allowing you to connect deeper with your community. Although the idea of going into business was at first intimidating, you become convinced it's where you're called to live your life of gratitude to your Higher Power.

So with much prayer and resolve, the first step you take is to commit this new business to your Higher Power's values and ways of doing things. In fact, you go so far (spiritually speaking) as to give over control and ownership of your business to this Higher Power and resolve to run it accordingly. You're simply the manager or steward of the gifts, talents, and resources that gave birth to your business.

True inner goodness and the Three-Legged Stool in business: quality, value, and service.

But now what? Where do you start?

125

Let's put aside your feelings of being overwhelmed and simply focus on what I call the Three-Legged Stool of business. It's not profound; actually, it's rather simplistic, yet any business venture that doesn't have all three legs will simply not thrive or even make it over the long haul.

The three legs are quality, value, and service.

Without quality, no matter how inexpensive the product or how great the service, no one will want your product. Your packaging may be engaging and your advertising glitzy and trendy, but eventually your customers will recognize the shoddy workmanship, and word will get around. Before long you'll find yourself sitting in your underwear at home, staring at the smartphone or tablet, wondering why no one is interested in what you're selling.

Without value (a fair price), even though the quality might be stupendous and your service outstanding, more than likely your clientele will be limited to the wealthy and elite who don't care how much it costs. Maybe if you get lucky and tap into a current fad, you can get away with overcharging for a while. However, in most cases, the market will catch up to you, someone else will take advantage of your high pricing, and you'll eventually get knocked down to earth.

Without service, even if your product is outstanding and your pricing remarkably fair, if you can't serve your customer and get it to them when they want or need it, they will go elsewhere, unless you're the only game in town and your customers have no choice. However, this will only persuade someone to enter your market and provide the service you're not supplying.

Quality, value, and service. Simple as that.

What's not so simple is being diligent about keeping these three in balance. It's imperative that we maintain our best quality while charging a fair price and getting the customer their product in a timely manner. This pretty much sums up the Golden Rule of treating others as you want to be treated.[1]

We sometimes overthink our business strategies. In today's cutthroat business climate, we often get caught up and distracted in looking for an edge, a way to get ahead of the competition by way of marketing and advertising to boost our sales or maybe a new technology or software that makes our business more efficient or trendy. However, neglect any part of the Three-Legged Stool, even for a moment, and you jeopardize the entire venture.

So let's get our fundamental processes and procedures in place before we get carried away with strategies and trends. Of course, marketing and advertising experts would argue there's no need for quality, value and service if, from the get-go, we don't figure out how to attract customers and persuade them to buy our product.

My counterargument is that you usually get only one shot at earning a loyal customer. Screw it up and they probably won't be back. Besides, if you truly have a legitimate product or service the world needs, my experience says that customers will find you with minimal advertising or marketing. In fact, if you provide kingdom-level quality, value, and service, your problem won't be finding customers but rather how to handle so many.

So how do we define quality, value, and service? Almost all companies today claim they provide all three, but words are cheap. Do they really? This is where the kingdom company has a distinct advantage in the marketplace. We aren't motivated just to make a quick and easy sale. Our convictions wouldn't allow it; true inner goodness doesn't allow it. We're called to a higher standard that Jesus ultimately modeled as He came not to start a new religion but to serve humanity, even to the point of death.

It's imperative to remember that our work isn't just for our benefit but for the good of others. The Three-Legged Stool of quality, value, and service is how we communicate God's higher standards and way of life. In other words, His kingdom. So we need to take all three very seriously.

QUALITY

Consider how *Merriam-Webster* defines quality: "peculiar and essential character," "an inherent feature," "degree of excellence," "superiority in kind."[2]

Do these definitions fit your product or service your business offers? Is quality the essential character and inherent feature? Is there a degree of excellence and superiority? Perhaps an even simpler question is, Are you proud of your product?

One of the supreme advantages the trades have over other professions is the ability to say at the end of the day, "Look what I made today!" Most tradespeople take enormous pride in the quality of their work and judge its quality not solely by its functionality but by its artistic and aesthetic qualities as well.

We often abhor the words "good enough." Whether it's a gear, a wooden cabinet, or a wiring or plumbing project, the tradespeople I respect the most are those who step back and admire their work. They have a personal commitment to making the best product possible, as if they're making it for royalty or a museum where it will be displayed for the entire world to see. As our journeymen train our apprentices, I often hear them ask the young machinist-in-training, "Would you buy this?" meaning the quality of their work needs to go beyond "good enough."

The question challenges our apprentices to treat our customers as they would want to be treated. Inferior craftsmanship is not an option. The gear may be functional, but if it's scratched up and not aesthetically pleasing to the eye, it's simply not acceptable.

Another aspect of quality is its enduring property. Will it last? How often have you bought something only for it to break in the first five minutes? Or the warranty was good for a year, and it broke at thirteen months? It seemed the manufacturer planned for it to fail to force you to buy another.

Do you want your customers to have the same experience and feelings of disgust? Wouldn't it be much more joyful if our customers were so thrilled with the quality and integrity of our products that they couldn't wait to tell others?

> **True inner goodness and *quality*: more than "good enough" and has an enduring property.**

Once again marketing and salespeople may argue that if our products last too long, we won't have enough sales. To this I say, Rubbish! Again, if your motivation is just to make a quick, one-time sale, you may have a point. But even then, your logic is faulty. The old adage of "It's much easier to keep a customer than to gain a new one" rings true. Supplying a product of superior, enduring quality is critical to long-term relationships.

In our gear business, we often have opportunities to provide options to our customers in terms of the materials and/or hardening processes used. Their engineers, out of simple ignorance, may have designed the gear using what we feel is an inferior material. When we explain how we can double or triple the life of the gear by making a few design changes at minimal cost, the choice is a no-brainer. Why wouldn't they want the gear to last longer?

Every once in a while, a customer will ask us if this is bad for our business. We usually explain it's just the opposite. When our customers discover we truly do have their best interests at heart, we not only have them for the long haul, but they become our sales force as they spread the word to others in their industry. It's been amazing to see how many purchasing agents and maintenance managers have brought us new customers, as they've changed jobs and convinced their new employers to buy their gears from us. There is no better sales lead than a referral from a happy customer.

Sounds simple, doesn't it? Yet I'm constantly amazed at how few understand such a simple concept.

VALUE

Let's look at how *Merriam-Webster* defines value: "a fair return or equivalent in goods, services, or money for something exchanged."[3]

It's commonly said that the worth of something is simply how much someone is willing to pay for it. Have you ever been to an auction? It can be entertaining, exciting, or frustrating, depending on whether you're a spectator or buyer. I've watched others get caught up in the thrill and competition of the bidding and end up paying ridiculous prices. It's not uncommon to see people buy something old and worn out for more than the cost of a new one. They usually didn't do their homework to see how much the new price was, and they got caught up in the moment. One man's junk can truly be another man's treasure.

But in business, should we actually charge as much as someone is willing to pay for it? Is this the value system we want to operate under? Many of our capitalist tendencies seem to endorse the "whatever the market will bear" approach to pricing. We often sing the praises of the free market system, but do we really want others to charge us as much as they can possibly get away with?

Of course the argument can be that we don't have to buy what they're offering. If we're foolish enough to pay what they're asking, it's our own fault, right?

Well let's look at it from a different perspective. What if you desperately needed something and there was only one business you could buy it from? What if it were insulin for your diabetic daughter, and your local pharmacy was the only supplier left in the county? What if they decided they wanted the mortgage to your house in exchange for it? Sound absurd?

In the past several years, there have been several news stories of drug companies doing almost exactly that. Knowing they had a corner on the market for one of their patented medications, they increased the price over 1,000 percent. For the poor patients, it was a matter of life and death, and they had to pay what the drug company charged. Eventually the company was made a public spectacle and shamed into lowering the price. But why did it have to get to that point?

Ultimately, how we price our products is a moral issue. It takes a tremendous amount of spiritual discipline and wisdom to charge the true and just value for our products and not just what someone will pay.

This raises the question: How do we determine the true value of our products?

I'm reminded of the quote by the famous founder of the Methodist movement, John Wesley. Christian business people should "gain all you can, save all you can, give all you can."[4] Wesley argued that Christians in business have a higher calling than just to make a profit. Today we might call it "capitalism with a conscience" or the "triple bottom line" of a company being socially, environmentally, and financially responsible.

Theologians, economists, and business experts have been debating the merits and dangers of capitalism for decades. The free market system can be a powerful force for prosperity for many, but devastating for others, as it seems we've been in an age of "predatory capitalism" for much longer than I've been alive.

However, taking advantage of others in the marketplace predates capitalism by centuries. I can imagine our ancestors thousands of years ago fighting over the best hunting grounds or berry patch. Has there ever been a period in human history where envy, jealousy, and greed weren't an issue?

So if we're going to seriously ask the question of how to price our products in business, in my opinion, it has to start by honestly examining our motives and hearts. As I've said earlier, money is an incredibly powerful force that easily corrupts all who come in contact with it. We can't be naïve and think our motives are always pure in our business dealings. I have yet to meet anyone in business who doesn't wrestle with money's corruptive influence.

Wait, let me rephrase that. If someone doesn't struggle with money's corruptive influence, they're already under its power. Put another way, if I'm not feeling more than a bit of conviction when my company is incredibly profitable, I get worried about the condition of my heart.

Yes, profit's good. Yes, when we treat our customers and

employees as we want to be treated, it's good for business. Yes, when we have a great product that the world genuinely needs, and we charge a fair price for it, the business tends to be very successful.

But under none of these circumstances do I have a right to charge our customers an excessive price that takes advantage of their need—period!

I know, I still haven't answered the question of what is a fair and just price for our products. The answer is different for everyone, but for the follower of Jesus, and any other citizen of the world with a moral compass, the answer is the same: as much as I need to make a necessary and honest profit so I may continue to serve our clients and care for our employees.

My business needs profit to survive and thrive but not so much profit to indulge our worldly appetites to the point of narcissism. It comes back to seeking the kingdom of God and His true inner goodness (righteousness). I'm not going to tell you how to price your products. That's up to you, God, and your customers. But it should be something you wrestle with every day. Treat others how you want to be treated. It's not that complicated, but it's a battle to keep our hearts pointed in the right direction.

One of the benefits of modern technology is the software that helps me analyze our business productivity and efficiencies. I can

True inner goodness and *value*: charging as much as is needed to make a fair and honest profit.

discover with a few clicks whether we made money or lost money on every single job that goes through our shop. Within seconds, I have a cost analysis report for any present or past job.

A good portion of our work is repeat business, meaning the

customer orders the same gear every few months or years. The customer will often request an updated quote, as we usually do need to raise our prices to keep up with the rising costs of wages, insurance, supplies, material costs, and so on. Generally, we raise our prices a modest 2–3 percent annually.

However, with the advent of new technologies, as well as the creativity and experience of our machinists, we can often find ways to reduce the manufacturing costs. It may actually cost less to produce the same gear today than it did five or ten years ago. So I requote a gear and discover our profit margin will be considerably higher than it was just a few years ago. Hooray! Right?

Well let's think about this. Should I simply continue to charge the customer more than I need to and keep the excess profits? They haven't complained about the price, so why should I rock the boat?

But what if the customer gets a quote from a competitor and gets a lower price? Wouldn't we be remiss in treating our customer fairly and be guilty of price gouging?

Some would argue, why worry about it? Charge as much as you can for as long as you can. My response to this is, "Stupid. Stupid. Stupid!" If we were the customer, is this how we would want to be treated? Jesus calls us to a higher standard. So as I requote the job and look at the cost history, I have to reconsider every single time if we're charging a fair price. Once again, wouldn't you like to be the customer who expects to pay the same price as last year or even a bit more—and then has the supplier respond that the price has actually gone down?

Besides having the pleasure of making our customers smile, I also sleep better at night having a clear conscience that we're doing our best to be fair.

That said, we must also be diligent in making sure we charge enough to be profitable. I actually know of good-hearted folks who feel guilty over charging a fair price for their products, and they don't charge enough.

Well guess what? It's hard to survive for very long if we view the whole world as a charity. There is nothing especially godly about not charging a fair price to make a profit so your business can survive and thrive. In fact, if your business is able to grow, you'll be able to serve that many more people and provide more meaningful employment. Profit's not a dirty word; in fact, it's not only good but absolutely essential for the survival of one's company.

SERVICE

Service is arguably not only the most important leg of the stool, but it's also, in my opinion, the distinguishing mark of a kingdom company that strives to embody and exhibit true inner goodness. It's one of the key aspects in business that can't be just talked about, studied, strategized, or listed on your website. It has to be real. Service is not just a critical aspect of our business model and one of the legs of our three-legged stool; it's a posture of our souls.

JESUS THE SMALL-BUSINESS GUY

By now, you hopefully are getting the message that Jesus is my ultimate role model for conducting business. Whether you were raised with a Christian education or not, most of us are aware of Jesus Christ as a major player in the world's religions.

Whether you're personally a follower of Jesus or an atheist

who thinks He's a mere man, there is no disputing the fact that His teaching (or the teachings attributed to Him) have been incredibly influential. Even Mahatma Gandhi respected and appreciated Jesus' teachings.

Whatever you may think you know or do not know about Jesus, one fact we often overlook is that He was a small-business guy who grew up in a family trade. Like all of us in business, He struggled with difficult customers, meeting deadlines, broken promises of vendors, and people not getting along. How do I know this? Some may argue I'm stretching things here, but when we carefully read the parables and His teachings, it's obvious He worked and lived in the real world and was not sequestered away like a monk in a religious retreat center.

Just a quick scan of His teachings in the book of Matthew shows He's in touch with everyday life, as He uses normal, everyday objects and experiences in His parables and illustrations. Salt, farming, fishing, taxes, lawsuits, difficult bosses, insects, rodents, handmade furniture, and lighting are just a few examples.

So, when He says that we're to go the extra mile, turn the other cheek, and be ridiculously generous when we're being sued, I personally believe He had some personal experience with all of this, as He and His dad plied their trade as wood workers, metal workers, and/or stone masons. Exemplifying true inner goodness and truly serving our customers is not easy, but it has a powerful impact, as I'm sure He learned.

> **True inner goodness and *service*: the distinguishing mark of a kingdom company.**

With all that said, there is one teaching of Jesus that stands out perhaps more than others, showing me He worked in business and lived with the frustration of constant broken promises by vendors and suppliers.

In the Jewish culture, having deep religious roots and traditions, it was common to make promises by swearing or pronouncing an oath, much like we do today. "I swear I'll be there tomorrow." "Honest to God, I'll call you right back." "On my mother's grave, I promise I'll pay you back."

As I get older, I become less tolerant of people's dramatic promises, as I'm confident Jesus did. Imagine Him showing up at a job site to frame in a door or put a roof over a well, and the mason, who was supposed to do the brick work ahead of Him, never showed up. Jesus had talked to the guy the week before, and the mason swore on his mother's grave that Jesus didn't need to worry. He promised the work would be done on time.

Jesus plans His work schedule, gathers materials and tools, loads up the donkey, and arrives to discover nothing has been done. Wouldn't you be a little ticked off?

Not just a little aggravated, He heads over to the boat yard to repair a fishing boat, but first must stop at the lumber yard to pick up several board feet of cedar that was promised Him. As the supplier has a tendency not to follow through, Jesus has pressed him the day before on whether the cedar would be ready. With stereotypical dramatic flair, the salesman said, "With God as my witness, Jesus, you can count on me." Jesus shows up, and no cedar.

Of course, I'm taking creative license here, but I imagine it was situations similar to these that prompted Jesus, to say,

"But I tell you, do not swear an oath at all: either by heaven, for it's God's throne; or by the earth, for it's his footstool; or by Jerusalem, for it's the city of the Great King. And do not swear by your head, for you cannot make even one hair white or black. All you need to say is simply 'Yes' or 'No'; anything beyond this comes from the evil one." (Matt. 5:34–37)

In other words, enough with your broken promises. Tell me the truth. Either you will do what you said or not. A simple yes or no will suffice.

Now, I'm about to give away perhaps the biggest secret to Edgerton Gear's success over the years. You might think I'm nuts for giving away our secrets, but I'm not in fear of anyone gaining a competitive advantage in this area. In fact, I'd be thrilled if all businesses would adhere to this one basic but absolutely critical principle.

If you gain nothing else from this book, let this be it. It has the power to make a bad company decent and a good company fantastic. If you can do this one simple thing, I believe you will outperform 99 percent of your industry. It's not complicated and is perhaps the easiest thing you can possibly do to be successful.

(Am I starting to sound like one of those internet ads that keep rambling on with the promise of the new miracle cure or way to get killer abs with no effort? Just keep reading and you'll learn our secret. And it will only cost you four easy payments of $39.99!)

It seems hardly anyone ever practices this secret anymore, so if you do it, you'll no doubt stand out from the crowd. We get numerous calls from our customers complimenting us on how we're one of their only vendors who do this regularly. Ready?

Got your highlighter out?

In the spirit of texting in capital letters to communicate shouting:

DO WHAT YOU SAY YOU'RE GOING TO DO!!!

It seems there is an epidemic in the business world of people simply not doing what they say they're going to do. I don't know about you, but I was taught at a very early age that if you don't do what you said you're going to do, you're a liar. No ifs, ands, or buts about it.

We're all busy and get interrupted; we're stressed and must struggle with the tyranny of the urgent. We all have good intentions, but the bottom line is if you can't keep your promises, DON'T MAKE THEM! (There I go again, I apologize for shouting, but I sometimes can't help myself.)

If you say you will call someone back, call them back. If you say you will visit your customer at 10 a.m. Thursday, visit them at 10 a.m. Thursday. If you say you will ship product tomorrow, make sure the product gets shipped tomorrow.

Granted, things can go wrong and emergencies beyond your control do happen. In these cases, be proactive and call the customer to explain. Most of the time, the customer is understanding and grateful for the call. It's when we don't call and leave expectations unmet that we fail to have a successful relational transaction.

Has it ever happened to you? Of course it has; it's happened to everyone. And how did this make you feel? Treat others as you want to be treated, and this starts by telling the truth!

Other gear shops that do not do what they promise are truly our best sales force. Edgerton Gear doesn't have a sales department, because new customers find us, often complaining that the other gear shops don't keep their promises of delivering on time. We can empathize with these complaints, as we've had numerous cases of our own vendors promising their work would be done by a certain date, only to discover on the due date that they haven't even started our order. We then have to call our customer and explain why we'll be late delivering their order, because our vendor lied to us.

As I said before, any breakdown in even one relational transaction jeopardizes the entire enterprise.

On the flip side of this argument, I should be thankful that the business world has an epidemic of lying and incompetence. It's the reason we're constantly busy with orders. So if you want to stand out and have a competitive edge, remember this one simple rule: do what you say you're going to do.

BULLET POINTS OF CUSTOMER SERVICE

Okay, I've *finally* gotten to the list of practical steps of service. You've hung in here this long, so I owe you this at least. In no particular order, here are the things we do to be successful in serving our customers.

- If at all possible, respond to emails within an hour or two.
- Answer the phone with a real person, not an automated system. I've come to despise automated answering services and will take my business elsewhere whenever possible.
- Quote your customer ASAP, preferably within hours, not longer than half a day.
- Quote realistic delivery dates. Don't lie to them to get the order.

- If situations arise that cause you to be late on the delivery, be proactive and call the customer to explain, giving them the new projected delivery date. Don't wait for the customer to call because the shipment didn't show up when you promised.
- Be fair in your pricing, not taking advantage of their crisis. It's fair and reasonable to charge an expedite fee, but again be reasonable. Don't try to make a fortune on one order.
- Treat the customer as you'd want to be treated.
- Don't take in work that doesn't fit your niche. If you do, be truthful with the customer and explain you'll be on a learning curve.
- Don't convince your customer to buy something they don't need. Truly listen to them and help them make good decisions based on what is best for them, not you.
- Pay your bills on time. Don't be like some companies who've adopted a strategy of making their customers pay quickly while they don't pay their vendors for months.
- Be committed to your customers' success. If you can think of ways to save them time and money, humbly ask if they're open to suggestions.
- Review your pricing always. If you've made a fair profit, great. If you've lost money, explore why and increase your pricing as needed, but explain why to your customer. If you made an excessive profit, reduce your price.
- Do whatever it takes to meet your customers' needs, especially in times of crisis. The last thing they want to hear when they have an emergency is, "Sorry, it's time for lunch," or, "We open tomorrow at eight."

- Communicate, communicate, and communicate. Don't trust emails and voicemail. In today's cyber world, we often rely too heavily on electronic media. Make sure your customer received the order acknowledgment, quote, or any other information they were looking for.
- Be patient, honest, kind, and respectful always—even if the customer isn't.

8

Burned Out or Fired Up?

"I miss my fun daddy!"

These weren't exactly the words I wanted to hear from my eight-year-old son at the time, but he was spot on. I often say the first two years of these past twenty-five were hellacious—and then things got worse.

I hadn't been the "fun daddy" for a very long time. In fact, home life had been downright scary at times. The pressures of taking over the family business were turning me into a monster. I was depressed, angry, and impossible to live with.

The past ten years of our journey had been excruciatingly painful and lonely. Out of the sixteen employees who were there when I took the reins from my father, now only five remained.

I had weathered betrayal, firing, hiring, and the removal of the pornography and keg of beer from the lunch room; I updated our technology by introducing computers; and I sought to foster a culture of trust, compassion, and community.

But at what price? My kids missed me, my wife was wondering if our marriage would survive, and my health was deteriorating. Was this the life God intended for us? Had He *really* called us back here, or was it our misguided imaginations?

I well remember the thoughts I wrote down on May 1, 1994:

Am I failing or succeeding? Perhaps that's the wrong question. Is God's will being done?

I hope so, but at this point in the journey, it's difficult to tell. For it has now been two years since I reentered the family business, full of faith, hope, and great expectations.

But the unrelenting tempest of misunderstandings, heart-wrenching conflicts, betrayals, accusations, etc., has taken its toll. I'm emotionally, physically, and spiritually spent.

SHAPING YOUR CALLING

Have you ever felt that God had abandoned you, that life could have turned out differently, and you should be doing something more significant in your career?

Maybe you're in a family business and feel trapped. Maybe your career has been a series of disappointments, never quite finding a sense of accomplishment or fulfillment. Maybe you currently feel stuck in a dead-end job with little hope for advancement or opportunity to grow.

If none of these circumstances apply to you, count yourself fortunate. However, I feel I'd be remiss if I didn't at least mention that the pain, frustration, and brokenness we often experience in life is not only part of our journey but can be a critical part of our calling—in other words, our life purpose.

For example, in the two years before we moved back to Wisconsin, I had the worst and best jobs of my life up to that point. The worst job was pouring concrete. I actually really enjoyed the physical part of the job and being part of laying the foundation for a house, garage, or apartment complex. Our work *mattered*.

However, my boss was a different story. Hands down, he was the meanest, angriest character I ever met. My last day on the job was the day he fired his brother and me for fixing his work from the day before.

We were roofing a pole shed as a filler job in between concrete jobs. If you know anything about roofing, if your first row is crooked, you have a royal mess just a few rows later. So we had to take a few hours to start over to correct the mistake.

When he showed up that afternoon, he blew a gasket, yelling and swearing at us because we weren't farther along. When we tried to explain we were fixing his rows, he got even more irate, packed up all the tools, and left us stranded on the roof. I looked at his brother and asked, "Were we just fired?"

He replied, "Appears so." I never heard from the boss again.

My best job, on the other hand, was the very next one, where I worked at a state park as an aide to the park rangers. Besides picking up trash and trimming trees, most of my time was spent cleaning bathrooms. I won't go into the disgusting details of what some people are capable of doing in terms of using their bodily functions as a tool for vandalism. But I'll say that to this day, I have an appreciation for the cleanliness of any public restroom.

Now the obvious question is, how could this possibly be the best job of my life up to that point? Besides being mostly outside with a view of the Puget Sound, I had the best boss and supervisors I had ever had. They respected and appreciated me, gave me lots of responsibility, trusted me, and were simply a joy to be around. The work itself had its ups and downs, but there was a genuine sense that we were serving the public—that we were behind the scenes making their experiences at a park gratifying and inspiring. We were contributing to the relational and physical health of their families and friends, as they enjoyed the profound sense of wonder and beauty of God's creation.

So what do both of these jobs have to do with my life purpose? If I believe that God has a major role in directing my life, it wasn't coincidental that these were the last two jobs I had before coming back to Edgerton Gear. Forever tattooed in my brain is the memory of being under the tyranny of a horrible boss versus how life-giving it was to work for a genuinely caring boss. It gave me a pretty clear idea of what kind of boss I wanted to be (and not be) when I came back to the shop. And this is just one small example of how our life experiences can shape us to fulfill our individual sense of calling.

God is at work shaping our life purpose.

Now you can argue that life is a series of unrelated coincidences. You can also say that your current job has no relation to your past jobs, and it's just plain good luck (or bad luck) that you're where you are now. You can even choose to believe there's no rhyme or reason to life at all. However, if you're still reading this, you don't really believe this to be the case. There are mysteries to life that can't be explained. There are no coincidences; someone else is in charge and it's not us.

So how have family, friends, jobs you've had, places you've lived, and all the other life experiences unique only to you shaped you and brought you to where you are now? A series of unrelated events? Of course not. I choose to think God is at work, even when others don't recognize it or believe it.

However, choosing to think this way doesn't mean it's easy and that our lives unfold in a fairy-tale sort of way, where we live happily ever after. On the contrary, believing that God is at work, and that we're where we're supposed to be, sometimes feels impossible, especially when life is seemingly unraveling before our eyes. How could it possibly be God's will that the stress of our jobs gets us to the point where we're ill, our spouses want to leave us, and our kids want nothing to do with us? Why would He allow us to suffer to this extent?

Or could it be that He has placed us in such situations for our own good, to foster our own personal growth, and possibly for the benefit of others as well? I have come to believe our lives are part of a much bigger story that is often beyond our understanding. A couple of illustrations from the Bible might be helpful.

Many of us have seen the Broadway show *Joseph and the Amazing Technicolor Dreamcoat*. It's based on the Old Testament story of Joseph in the book of Genesis, starting at chapter 39. Yes, Joseph was an annoying little brother. He had some crazy dreams, in which his brothers would someday bow down to him. No, he didn't have to tell his brothers those dreams—but he did. And yes, his dad wasn't helpful by showing favoritism toward him. But throwing him in a pit, selling him as a slave, and then faking his death, as his brothers did? Yeah, I think he had a couple of emotional scars.

Or how about when Moses was miraculously saved from

infanticide so he could someday lead his people out of slavery? Read that story beginning in Exodus 2. I tend to imagine he slowly recognized he was different from others in Pharaoh's household, and there was a reason he was raised and educated as royalty. Did he carry a weight of destiny only to kill an abusive Egyptian and run for his life? He then spent forty years in the boondocks as a shepherd before God tells him to return to Egypt. What lessons did his job teach him to prepare him to lead a group of city-dwelling slaves through the wilderness for the next forty years?

In our modern world, we sometimes mistakenly assume that if we seek to do the right thing and honor God in all we do, we'll be "blessed." I have no doubt we'll *eventually* be blessed, but it may or may not be in this lifetime.

In fact, the path to being blessed may not remotely *resemble* anything like a blessing. My experience tells me hardship is perhaps the only way to deepen our character and mold us into being the people God intended us to be, as the above examples illustrate.

For whatever reason, pain, suffering, failure, and loss seem much better teachers than pleasure and success. If we truly intend to be vessels of God's true inner goodness, it means abandoning and surrendering ourselves to God, and trusting He will make some sense of the pain and chaos.

BACK TO THE SCENE OF THE "CRIME"

I think back to one of my mentors, Gerry, when we first returned to Wisconsin. The only job Gerry ever had was the family bakery, and he struggled through the legacy of alcoholism, much as I did.

One of the "Gerryisms" that has permeated my theology is "God always brings us back to the scene of the crime."

Gerry contends that we often have times and places in our lives that leave wounds and scars, and it's only by revisiting those places that we can find some semblance of healing and wholeness. For Gerry, it meant staying in the family bakery for decades, wrestling with his own demons in the family business as a child of an alcoholic. For me, it was coming back to Edgerton Gear, the place I swore I'd left forever.

The obvious question is, why? Why would God bring us back to these painful places?

Answers are rarely simple and one-dimensional. On a macro level, it might simply be part of God's bigger plan. On the micro level, it might be for our own good to face and deal with our past wounds. Being wounded by others can scar us in numerous ways. Despair, bitterness, self-worthlessness, an over-developed sense of importance, or a desperate need for significance can cripple us in ways we're often not even aware of, which can lead us to inflicting the same wounds on others that were inflicted on us.

The antidote, as the Good Physician knows, is often revisiting these places, recognizing how we were wounded, and then seeking healing and wholeness.

Can you imagine how painful it was for Joseph to face his brothers, who had committed the heinous act of human trafficking? Sure, he had saved Egypt and his family during a prolonged and devastating drought. But how big

Being God's vessels of true inner goodness means trusting Him to make sense of our life journey.

of a hole did Joseph have in his heart after being abandoned and sold by his own brothers decades before? No one ever gets over such trauma, and I have to believe Joseph's pain drove him to be incredibly successful and accomplished.

Forty years prior to Moses being called by God at the burning bush, he struck down an Egyptian and was consequently rejected by his own people. But God sent him back to lead the exodus. How deep was his insecurity and self-doubt, as he spent four decades as a shepherd before God told him to return to the literal scene of the crime?

Both men were pivotal in God's grand design of reconciling all nations to himself. It had to be extremely painful for both men to revisit their past, but it was necessary in light of God's greater purposes. Scripture shows us how Joseph wept upon meeting his brothers.

A story from the gospels deepens this point. In Mark 5, we read the story of Jesus delivering a demon-possessed man, who had been horribly tormented. The locals tried to bind him with chains to subdue him. "Night and day among the tombs and in the hills he would cry out and cut himself with stones" (Mark 5:5).

After Jesus set him free, the people of the region, either because of fear, anger, or disbelief, begged Jesus to leave. More than likely they felt that Jesus was bad for the pork industry, since the demons went into a herd of pigs and ran them off a cliff. Regardless, Jesus left behind a witness.

"As Jesus was getting into the boat, the man who had been demon-possessed begged to go with him. Jesus did not let him, but said, 'Go home to your family and tell them how much the Lord has done for you, and how he has had mercy on you.' So the man went away and began to tell in the Decapolis how much

Jesus had done for him. And all the people were amazed" (Mark 5:18–20).

What a miserable existence this man must have lived prior to being delivered, as the ridicule, rejection, and loneliness must have been unbearable. Not only was he in a position to testify of God's mercy and power to a community that needed mercy, but for his own good, he needed to forgive them as well. So he was left behind to face those who tried to bind him in chains.

Whether we realize it or not, we all have a need to know that God can heal our deepest wounds. It's often in the places we find uncomfortable or even impossible that God does some of His best work. Your role and the circumstances in your business may be uncomfortable and even impossible, but without you knowing it, God is doing remarkable work *in* you and *through* you. Rather than fight it like I did for many years, maybe it's time to yield to it and embrace the place God has you.

BE THE CHANGE—JUST NOT BY YOURSELF

I tend to think most of us in the business world don't have any notion of a calling or a life purpose until we're well into our careers—maybe even never. The majority of us were more concerned about supporting our families and just having a job we didn't hate. If we actually enjoyed our work, that was just an added bonus.

The stuff of life when we're young, such as getting a car, house, family, and maybe living in a new place, with new people to befriend and work with, tends to take up most of our time and energy. We just followed where the career opportunities opened. The few people who have known what they wanted to do with their lives since they were in fifth grade are the exceptions.

However, I have yet to meet anyone who doesn't long to have a sense that their lives matter and that they're doing something meaningful. Reality sometimes bites, as we often feel we're barely surviving in our work world, holding on for dear life as pressures, temptations, and boredom wear us down. Can this be part of our calling? Is God quietly at work in all of us, prodding and guiding us on a path that enlists our gifts and talents? Are some of us actually living out our calling and not even realizing it? Do we have any sense of a greater purpose or divine destiny?

> **In seeking God's kingdom and His true inner goodness, He doesn't promise me happiness, but He does ask for my persevering obedience.**

For me, one of the greatest challenges of being called to business is not being convinced that God called me to come back to the shop. It's *staying* convinced that God wants me to stay here.

The workplace is not for the faint of heart. Growing up, I watched what the stress did to my dad, and my sons have seen what it has done to me. I've endured multiple cycles of burnout, when I became exhausted, sometimes leading to severe illness. I'd often behave out of character, such that I knew I needed to make drastic changes. I'd then get better for a while, but the stress would come back, as the business grew and new challenges overwhelmed me.

My wife knows I'm on the edge again when my fuse is short or I start daydreaming of packing up a few survival tools and moving into the wilderness, where nobody can find me. I think the American version of Christianity has often skewed my understanding of what it means to be called by God, because I somehow expect and even demand that this calling to business shouldn't be so hard. But God always reminds me that nothing worthwhile is ever easy.

In seeking God's kingdom and His true inner goodness, He doesn't promise me happiness, but He does ask for my persevering obedience. *This* is a big part of my calling.

What is particularly exciting is that I don't have to figure out how to do this by myself. Jesus repeatedly makes it clear that He is the source of true inner goodness and of life itself. God will empower and enable us to exhibit that true inner goodness. As He says,

> I'm the Vine, you are the branches. When you're joined with me and I with you, the relation intimate and organic, the harvest is sure to be abundant. Separated, you can't produce a thing. (John 15:5 MSG)

Don't believe me? Or maybe you'd like to believe what I'm saying, but it sounds too good to be true? Well, people a lot smarter than I am have been trying to get this message across for years. Paul Stevens, in his marvelous work *Doing God's Business*, says it much better than I can, so allow me to quote him extensively on this topic.

> I think [the apostle] Paul, if he were writing to business-people today, might say something like this:
>
> Stay in your business but go deep. Your work station, your office, your position will teach you everything

and will be a means of growth in faith. Don't think that going into religious work will be a spiritual advantage. Your life is not a bundle of accidents. All the things that led you to where you're now—birth, education, interests, advantages, and opportunities —are part of God's providential leading in your life. Where you were when God called you is significant and is taken up into the all-embracing summons of God. Your life and daily work are significant and, if done not for yourself but unto the Lord, will not be in vain.[1]

> **Your life circumstances and journey are unique. No one else in the world can fill your shoes as a vessel of God's true inner goodness.**

Stevens goes on to point out that there is not one instance of anyone in the Bible being called to business, "nor is there a single instance of a person being called to be a religious professional."[2]

I hope by now that as you reflect on your own life circumstances and journey, it's starting to sink in how unique your position is and that no one else in the world can fill your shoes. There is no one else who has the same experiences growing up with your parents, siblings, friends, schools, jobs, successes, failures, heartaches, challenges that broke you, shaped you, and strengthened you. No one else has your temperament, interests, gifts, talents, likes, dislikes, perspectives, and passions.

If you're part of a family business, chances are you have more wisdom and common sense about the business than you realize. Things that you take for granted or that you think your staff should know are often difficult concepts and skills for them to grasp and learn. If you're established in a career working in a small or large business, you have skills and tribal knowledge that you've acquired over a lifetime that can't be taught in a few years of college.

You have the ability to bring clarity to complex problems simply because you've been around the block a few times. For you to leave your position because you feel "called to ministry" (as in paid, professional religious work), means you might be failing to appreciate the current role God has you in.

Now, if you're bored in your job and need a change, that might be another matter altogether. But it could still be because you can't see the bigger picture in the role you serve, in other words, how you're already doing ministry where you are. Or it might actually be time for a change, and God is leading you elsewhere.

However, don't discount a whole lifetime of experiences God has built into your life. Your life purpose, or calling, as Stevens says above, encompasses all of you: your past, present, and future. The longer you stay in your career or industry, the more street credibility you earn. People begin to recognize your experience, wisdom, and staying power. I've come to the conclusion that a calling is not so much about a specific occupation as it is a posture or response to God summoning us to join Him in His ministry, or service to the world. In this context, our businesses becomes an extension or manifestation of what is often called our interior life. If you're called to embrace Jesus' summons to join God, your business cannot *not* be part of your calling.

As willing participants in God's rule, and as champions of His desire to mend our broken world, we can, to quote a popular slogan, "be the change."

In whatever situation or sphere of influence we occupy, God desires to display samples of His kingdom through us. As the apostle Paul states in his second letter to the Corinthians, "All this is from God, who reconciled us to himself through Christ and gave us the ministry of reconciliation" (5:18). In practical terms, we're it. We're the agents of God's mercy, grace, love, justice, and truth. We're the conduit through whom God wants to heal the world.

> **"There is no arena, however demonic, to which one cannot be called by God to minister."**
> —*Richard Broholm*

When His righteousness, His true inner goodness, oozes out of us, it changes things. Like a magical formula or tonic, when people encounter true inner goodness, they can't help but be affected by it. Either they rebel against it, or they're drawn to it and changed. God desires the entire world to experience it, but it's a tremendous job, bigger in scope than we can imagine, too big for the religious professionals.

So the brilliance of the plan is to anoint every follower of Jesus to be a minister (i.e., a servant) and for them to penetrate every corner of society to reclaim and reorder people, places, and processes under God's sovereign rule by allowing His true inner goodness to flow through them.

No job and no place are off limits. We're needed everywhere, in gear shops and cafes, in libraries and HVAC companies, in paper mills and offices. Every part of what makes a civilization tick needs the touch of God to bring it in line with how God intended. As Richard Broholm says, "There is no arena, however demonic, to which one cannot be called by God to minister."[3]

So it's difficult to define or describe what the kingdom of God would be like for every person, because it would be different in every situation. How the kingdom of God and His righteousness comes through a plumber is different from how it comes through a prison warden, which is different from how it comes through an elementary schoolteacher, which is different from how it comes through a homemaker, farmer, lawyer, machinist, and so on.

The world is broken. From a purely humanistic, secular standpoint, we all have to ask ourselves if we're part of the problem or part of the solution. Which side are you on? Are you helping to make things better or worse? It's a simple question we ask our shop kids.

The greater we grow in our affluence and influence, the greater our responsibility and potential to do harm or good. Add to this the religious element of hooking our wagon up to God and His infinite power of creativity and mysterious ability to work in and through us, and we become little dynamos to bring healthy change to all spheres of life simply by humbly doing our jobs and allowing His true inner goodness to flow from us in all situations and decisions.

Go watch the classic American movie *It's a Wonderful Life*, as George Bailey unwittingly embodies the power of a life of faithful and humble service. I have no doubt there are thousands upon thousands of George Baileys in our communities who are rarely recognized but are faithfully playing a vital role in God's kingdom. You're probably one of them. Sometimes the difference between being burned out and fired up is nothing more than having the right perspective.

9

What Makes a Leader?

"When you don't lead, we all suffer."

I didn't want to hear it, but he was right; the shop had lost focus. Everyone seemed distracted. Our scrap was up, production was down, and the staff was bickering in response to a general sense of tension in the air. And it was my fault. Once again, like other times in the past, the stress of being in charge had worn me down, and I had withdrawn into my cocoon. I didn't want to solve any more problems, hear anyone's complaints, or be responsible for anything. I was burned out and needed to shut down and recharge.

Yet my shop manager's words hit me hard when he gently said those words I've quoted.

You may not own your own business or be in a formal position of leadership in your workplace, but in small or grand ways, you most likely have known what it is to lead or be led. Although this chapter focuses primarily on leadership in the workplace, the principles apply everywhere.

For me, leadership is one of the great mysteries of life. Some people have it, others simply don't. Some folks who thought they were great leaders were not, while some who didn't think they were leaders at all were terrific. Sometimes, the person who is most qualified to lead gets shoved aside by a person who simply has a stronger personality.

In high school, the athletes who blossomed physically before everyone else sometimes became leaders by default, being bigger and stronger than their classmates. This didn't necessarily make them good leaders, which they painfully discovered in adulthood. Other kids who were late to the party of adolescence, and were bullied and humiliated into believing they were inferior, sometimes became incredible leaders after the tyranny of high school.

The health and effectiveness of your workplace is 100 percent tied to the health and effectiveness of the leaders.

Some leaders are leaders because of their position of authority, such as their job title or rank. Some leaders gain authority because of their years of experience and expertise. Still some leaders have neither rank, position, expertise, nor experience, yet people are naturally drawn to follow them.

I'm not going to pretend to understand any of this. Besides, there are hundreds of books that go into great detail on the topic to explain what leadership is and is not. But what I do know is that any leader, from the captain of a softball team to a coordinator of a book club to the president of the United States to a parent to a business owner, has in his or her possession the power to do both great things and horrible things. Leadership is power demanding stewardship and respect from those who wield it. In business, one's leadership has more to do with the success or failure of a venture than any other factor.

Now I'll leave it to the experts to define all the critical elements of leadership, such as "a leader needs followers." Even this simple

> **The toxicity and ineffectiveness of the leaders is directly tied to how dysfunctional and ineffective the workplace will be.**

fact doesn't mean you're a great, or even good leader. At the very least, all it means is that people are gullible or desperate enough to follow. Hitler was a great leader, and so were numerous cult leaders over the centuries.

What we're after here is the type of leadership that is a vessel of God's kingdom and His true inner goodness.

At this point, my writing skills are a great source of frustration because I can't come up with the right words to convey how important this next point is. I'd love to sit down with you, look you straight in the eye and convince you that there is nothing more important to your business than this: *The health and effectiveness of your workplace is 100 percent tied to the health and effectiveness of the leaders.* Period.

Conversely, *the toxicity and ineffectiveness of the leaders is directly tied to how dysfunctional and ineffective the workplace will be.*

You may argue that I'm being a bit dramatic, since there are plenty of businesses that seem to be doing fine, and the leaders are not pillars of emotional health and virtue. I know quite a few of these companies myself. It seems no matter how poorly these leaders treat their vendors and staff, and even their customers, the firms are still thriving.

You probably know someone like Bill (not his real name, of course) who has such a reputation. People either hate him or love him. Come to think of it, even those who supposedly love him admit he is one of the most arrogant people on the planet. Yet his company continues to grow and is considered a great success. (Just ask him.)

But, as you know by now, if we're striving to be followers of Jesus, our success isn't measured just by the bottom line of dollars and cents. Success isn't measured by the triple or even quadruple bottom line of profit, people, planning, and purpose, which are all incredibly important. No, we're called to surpass all of the world's measurements and exhibit a level of goodness that isn't even attainable without God's intervention and guidance.

Impossible standards? Absolutely! But I don't recall anywhere in Jesus' teaching that tells us to be average. In fact, in Jesus' teaching on the Sermon on the Mount, before He says His famous words about seeking God's kingdom and His righteousness, He gives multiple examples of exceeding what is expected.

Remember our previous discussion of loving our neighbor? In Matthew chapter 5, we are told to love not only our neighbors but our enemies as well, and even pray for them. Jesus then says, "Be perfect, therefore, as your heavenly Father is perfect" (v. 28).

Again, impossible standards! But that's the point. Jesus wants to redefine goodness, to reorientate our ideas of success. Eventually, none of the world's measurements will matter. We can take no amount of wealth, power, market share, influence, or affluence to the grave. And I'm not being morbid, just honest.

As the apostle Paul, who was a pretty successful but nasty guy before Jesus got hold of him, says in his famous letter to the Corinthians in chapter 13 (which is almost always read at weddings), when it's all said and done, all that's left is faith, hope, and love.

Basically, God is infinitely more concerned with who we become than with what we accomplish. It therefore stands to reason that our workplaces are not only a powerful force for goodness in the form of goods, services, and employment, but they also serve as our refining fire, making us better people and exposing our greed, envy, prejudices, selfishness, and other self-destructive behaviors.

As mentioned earlier, there's no place to hide in the workplace; our badness or foul motives will be exposed. We

> **God is infinitely more concerned with who we become than with what we accomplish.**

will fail, flounder, and disappoint. But it's in these moments, just like when a journeyman is teaching an apprentice, where our shortcomings become opportunities to learn and grow, where God can make us better vessels of His true inner goodness.

So what does this have to do with leadership, and specifically leadership in the workplace? Think for a moment how you'd define a godly leader. Who do you know who exemplifies true inner goodness in their business dealings, who consistently treats others as they themselves would want to be treated? Maybe it's you and you don't even realize it, but I'm sure your instincts, your gut feelings, know who does and doesn't model virtuous leadership. Let's compare and contrast a couple of real life examples.

I just got off the phone with Laura, who is in the middle of buying another business and is trying to get the lay of the land and connect with all the parties who have a stake in the transaction. Laura asked me what I thought of Mitch, who is not directly involved with the business, but will be impacted by the transaction.

I hesitated to answer, because I didn't want to cloud or influence her decision or perception of another business person. However, Laura immediately picked up on my hesitation. Neither of us wanted to slander Mitch, because we both believed he is a good guy. But in the end, we both admitted neither of us would ever go into business with him. Why? Mitch is out for Mitch.

Mitch always gives the impression that money, success, and getting a deal are his top priorities. Laura, on the other hand, never gives the slightest hint that making money is her top priority. On the contrary, she is very savvy and strategic; it's clear what's driving her ambition is more than the challenge of buying and building a business. She is passionate about relationships and that all parties are valued, respected, and engaged.

Of course, this makes good business sense, but it's more than that. Laura inspires trust and enthusiasm to follow her. Mitch has a way about him that causes you to keep a hand on your wallet and your mouth shut when you're around him. You sense he's constantly looking for an advantage.

This comparison isn't profound or unusual. We can all point out the Lauras and Mitches in our work worlds. The questions are, which one do you want to be? And why does it matter?

The first answer is obvious, as it's a rhetorical question. If you're reading this book, you realize that, *of course*, you don't want to be Mitch. *Mitch* probably doesn't want to be Mitch and would probably be devastated if he knew Laura and I felt this way about him. Yet he is sending out a vibe that he is selfish and can't be trusted.

So why does it matter? Because God made us to be in relationships with each other, and leaders have a profound influence on the quality of relationships. These relationships are an extension of your interior life. As Jesus said, "What comes out of the mouth gets its start in the heart.

> **Leaders have a profound influence on the quality of relationships. These relationships are an extension of your interior life.**

It's from the heart that we vomit up evil arguments, murders, adulteries, fornications, thefts, lies, and cussing. That's what pollutes" (Matt. 15:18–19 MSG).

In other words, who you are on the inside will determine whether you vomit on others or bless them. So as a leader in your workplace, no amount of business strategy, benefits, wage packages, or customer service policies can take the place of a pure and clean heart.

Let me try to explain it in another way. One of the most profound books I've read in the last decade or so is by the late Edwin Friedman, an ordained Jewish rabbi, a family systems therapist, and a consultant on leadership and organizations. He spent most of his career studying human relationships and what dynamics make them healthy and unhealthy. The first book I read of his, *Generation to Generation*,[1] was literally life changing for me, as it helped me understand what was really behind the dysfunction of our family business and how I could not only address it but hopefully bring a level of health to it.

However, his final book, *A Failure of Nerve: Leadership in the Age of the Quick Fix*,[2] was a culmination of his life's work. Unfortunately, he unexpectedly died before he was able to finish his last chapters. But then again, maybe it was meant to be. Friedman would probably want to leave us hanging so we would be able to draw our own conclusions, like a Jedi master leaving room for an apprentice to find their own way.

Fortunately for us, Friedman's daughter gathered up his notes and published what he had completed. To me, the book is a treasure. It reminds me of the classic cartoon of a pilgrim strenuously climbing the highest mountain to seek the wisdom of the sage who is sitting at the very top, meditating. The sage is old and wise from his years of experience, and every word that comes from his mouth is like a drop of gold. Friedman's last book is kind of like this to me: After years of learning, teaching, and consulting, what did he ultimately learn and want to share in his last days?

In his own words,

Leadership in America is stuck in the rut of trying harder and harder without obtaining significant new results . . . The way out, rather, requires shifting our orientation to the way we think about relationships, from one that focuses on techniques that motivate others to one that focuses on the leader's own presence and being.[3]

In other words, who you are as a person is much more important than all the latest management techniques and strategies to lead and motivate people. Breaking this down to the most basic question, we need to ask ourselves, "Am I a good person?" Now this is where it gets interesting. If you took an informal survey of everyone you know, including family members, friends, and coworkers, and asked them whether they think they're basically a good person, how many would respond and say: "Nope. Not really. I'm bad"?

None of them, right? If they did, you should probably keep your distance. All of us tend to think we're basically good people at heart. The problem is, we're masters of self-deception, and "good" is a very relative term. One person may think he's good because he doesn't kick his dog or beat the children. Another may think she's good because she regularly attends church. Still others would define goodness with the

> **Virtues are the foundations for our businesses, which, are extensions of our inner beings, our interior lives.**

old jingle from the 1950s: "Don't drink, smoke, swear, or chew or go out with those who do!"

I would argue that not kicking your dog or beating your children are the only ones that even hint at the condition of your heart. The others may be little more than keeping up appearances when others are looking.

Being truly good digs much deeper, as we covered earlier in our lengthy discussion on righteousness and true inner goodness. It's about the universal, virtuous character qualities that determine how we live. Or, as David Gill puts it in *Becoming Good*, "Virtues are the skills needed to accomplish the tasks of life."[4]

These virtues are also the foundations for our businesses, which, to repeat myself, are extensions of our inner beings, our interior lives. You might say they're character in action. Words such as *humble, trustworthy, cooperative, respectful, disciplined, fair, courageous,* and *honest* are not theoretical words we can claim will describe us without proof.

And seeing that we tend to be biased in describing whether we're truly good or not, the only real proof is how others who know us and interact with us would describe us. For example, in our Craftsman with Character class, after our students assemble their own lists of virtuous character qualities, we require them to ask their family members and close friends to honestly tell them how they measure up. Goodness is proven by action in relationship to others.

So why is *goodness* important for a leader? As Friedman learned after decades of working with all types of organizations, such as synagogues, churches, and businesses, it's the very presence of the leader that counts, not what he or she knows. "Leaders function as the immune system of their institutions," he writes. The ultimate difference will not be in how they exercise power, "how well their *presence* is able to preserve . . . integrity."[5]

I don't know about you, but when I read this, I can't help but say, "Wow! Let's read that again. And I invite you to go back one paragraph and do just that. Isn't that what we all secretly want—for a leader to preserve integrity? To be a person of integrity we can trust? To keep everyone's best interests at heart? To always strive to do the right thing? Isn't this what Jesus was talking about in the Sermon on the Mount, when He talked about goodness?

In other words, our goodness must exceed that of the religious professionals. Jesus implied someone could be a prostitute, a tax collector, or anyone else society looks down upon, but still have more goodness, more integrity than those who simply *pretend* to have integrity. Sooner or later, our deep-down identity manifests itself on what we do on the surface.

Our actions matter, as they represent the conditions of our hearts. In leadership, the actions rooted in our hearts speak louder than catchy slogans, mission statements, and fluffy motivational speeches.

One of the things I appreciate the most about blue-collar tradespeople is what I call their *biker mentality*. Wisconsin is home to Harley

> **"The crucial issue [for a leader is] . . . how well their presence is able to preserve integrity.**
> —*Edwin Friedman*

Davidson motorcycles, and it's not unusual for machinists to be bikers. You've probably heard their bikes before you've seen these riders, with their black leather outfits, often long hair and/or shaved heads. They tend to look very intimidating. They're fiercely independent and mistrust anything to do with "The Man," which is usually referring to those in positions of higher authority who represent the establishment of government and big business and who impose their values on these independent souls.

What I've come to love about them is how much they value sincerity and authenticity. They have no respect or patience for anyone who tries to impress others or use manipulation as a way to get ahead. They can be a challenging lot to have in your work force, because they tend to see right through phoniness and will question everyone's motives.

However, once you have their trust, which has to be earned by sincere good action, they're incredibly loyal. I've come to realize they hold me accountable to leading with integrity, to model integrity, and to preserve integrity throughout the organization. And the only way to lead with this depth of integrity is to constantly be aware of my own integrity, or lack thereof.

Friedman would have me focus not on how I manage the shop, but how I manage myself. The fancy term he uses is *well-differentiated*. If I'm healthy emotionally, relationally, and spiritually, the business will follow suit. If I'm insecure, needy, egotistical, manipulative, selfish, and/or a people pleaser, the entire organization will feel the effects.

> **To be *well-differentiated* is to focus and be aware of my health and goals. The more I take care of myself, the healthier the organization becomes.**

The symptoms might be constantly putting out fires, too many people needing a shoulder to cry on, the refereeing of petty disputes, and trying to get everyone to like me and each other. A general malaise of insecurity, chaos, and apathy takes hold. Rather than tackle these symptoms, Freidman instructs me to be *well-differentiated*, to focus and be aware of my health and goals. It might sound counterintuitive and even self-centered, but the more I take care of myself, the healthier the organization becomes. This same principle applies at home with the family, coaching the kids' soccer team, and organizing a school fundraiser. The healthier I am emotionally, the better it is for those I'm interacting with.

Friedman doesn't mean for us to be aloof and unconnected to others. On the contrary, he says we need to be "someone who can separate while still remaining connected, and therefore can maintain a modifying, non-anxious, and sometimes challenging presence."[6]

If you want a pretty clear example of the type of leader that Friedman describes, take your time reading the Gospels and notice how Jesus fits the above criteria. He has clarity about His life goals (bringing God's kingdom to earth). He doesn't get lost in everyone's anxieties, emotional gymnastics, or their freaking out to decide whether He is or isn't the Messiah. He stays incredibly connected to everyday folks and His disciples, yet withdraws when He needs to be alone.

He is a *very* challenging presence, yet seems never to be anxious when opposed. When threatened, He doesn't over-react. He stays the course, even when He displeases and disappoints almost everyone.

What I find especially fascinating is that Friedman's description of the qualities of the best leaders are remarkably similar to what Jim Collins describes in his bestseller *Good to Great: Why Some Companies Make the Leap—and Others Don't*.[7] Collins and his team selected eleven large corporations that far outperformed every other company over a fifteen-year period. Most of us can't relate to what goes on in big corporate America, but Collins's research provides some invaluable lessons for all businesses. In fact, our gear shop held a mandatory book club shortly after the book came out, and we discussed it in monthly breakfast meetings.

Many of the lessons are common sense in the workplace, especially for those of us in the trades and manufacturing. But it was extremely helpful and affirming to see the importance of what we intuitively already know, such as the value of discipline, good people, honesty, and integrity, as well as getting the right people in the right places and the wrong people "off the bus," so to speak.

I consider the book a must-read for anyone in business. Not surprisingly, leadership plays a huge role. What is surprising is what *kind* of leadership.

Collins discovered that what set certain CEOs apart— "Level 5 Leaders," as he calls them—was not their charisma or ambition. He says these exceptional captains of industry are "a study in duality: modest and willful, humble and fearless."[8] They don't draw attention to themselves, but are humbly passionate about their company. "The good-to great leaders never wanted to become larger-than-life heroes. They never aspired to be put on a pedestal or become unreachable icons. They were seemingly ordinary people quietly producing extraordinary results."[9]

Take a look at Collins's summary of what Level 5 Leadership looks like. Professional Will is committed to the success of the company while Personal Humility recognizes a leader is not the center of the universe and is committed to the success of others.

Remember the two jobs I described in the last chapter about the worst and best bosses I ever had, one working in concrete and the other in a state park? They're also examples of the two extremes of leadership we often see in business today. The concrete boss represents the bigger-than-life personality who is strong, outspoken, opinionated, arrogant, ruthless, and incredibly anxious. When things went wrong, he was quick to blame others and rarely gave praise for a job well done.

THE TWO SIDES OF LEVEL 5 LEADERSHIP
(Jim Collins)[10]

PROFESSIONAL WILL	PERSONAL HUMILITY
Creates superb results, a clear catalyst in the transition from good to great.	Demonstrates a compelling modesty, shunning public adulation; never boastful.
Demonstrated an unwavering resolve to do whatever must be done to produce the best long-term results, no matter how difficult.	Acts with quiet, calm determination; relies principally on inspired standards, not inspiring charisma, to motivate.
Sets the standard of building an enduring great company; will settle for nothing less.	Channels ambition into the company, not the self; sets up successors for even greater success in the next generation.
Looks in the mirror, not out the window, to apportion responsibility for poor results, never blaming to other people, external factors, or bad luck.	Looks out the window, not in the mirror, to apportion credit for the success of the company to other people, external factors, or good luck.

The park boss, being an example of a Level 5 Leader, was very strong, yet soft spoken, valued other's opinions, was humble, thoughtful, and usually relaxed—always grateful for our efforts. The first instilled fear and anxiety while the other inspired trust, hard work, and excellence.

Corporate America has probably had more of the former than the latter, but there is a growing awareness that being a jerk doesn't work so well.

WHO ARE YOU?

Chances are you've exhibited most of the qualities of a Level 5 leader, whether at work, at home, or in any organization you've served in. In my experience, most of us don't go to work to get rich quick and to live lifestyles of the rich and famous. We have a skill or service that the world needs, and we are good at providing it.

Many of us (not all) don't enjoy the spotlight and attention. We simply want to do our jobs and are passionate about doing it well. Drawing on the theme of true inner goodness, we intuitively know what good leadership looks like and the virtuous character qualities it requires.

However, where most of us get hung up (and Freidman, I'm sure, would heartily agree) is the last part, about looking in the mirror. It takes a great degree of deep humility and personal awareness to avoid being toxic.

As leaders, are we truly aware of how we affect other people? When things go bad, do we accuse or blame others? Do we become cynical, moody, and broody, sending out a vibe that signals everyone to stay clear? When things go well, do we take the credit and demand a pat on the back? Or do we give credit to everyone and everything but ourselves?

One of the best quotes I've ever read on leadership is from Max De Pree's masterpiece, *Leadership is an Art*: "Leaders don't inflict pain; they bear pain." [11]

Think for a moment of all the bosses or leaders you've worked with. Like many from my generation, I had a lot of different jobs in my youth. I mowed lawns, weeded gardens, harvested and stripped tobacco, cut and split firewood, drove a bus, worked in retail, and others. Without exception, my memories of those jobs are either fond, bitter, or indifferent mostly because of who my boss was.

Did he or she inflict pain or bear pain when I screwed up? Did he or she patiently teach, en-

> **"Leaders don't inflict pain; they bear pain."**
> —*Max De Pree*

courage, and inspire me? Or was he or she a tyrant, making me feel inept, stupid, and uninspired?

I might add that these experiences shaped how I viewed parenting. During those moments when I was less than the ideal dad, it was helpful to reflect back on the effect these leaders/bosses had on me. What kind of leader was I being to my sons?

Over the years since those earlier jobs, I've watched how leaders interact with those they're supposedly leading, and it's pretty easy to know how healthy a leader he or she is based on how they make others feel.

As De Pree continues, "The measure of leadership is not the quality of the head, but the tone of the body. The signs of outstanding leadership appear primarily among the followers. Are the followers reaching their potential? Are they learning? Serving? Do they achieve the required results? Do they change with grace? Manage conflict?"[12]

Again, we can see how this applies to all relationships where we are looked upon as a leader, especially within a family.

At this point, if you have even a speck of humility and honesty, you may recognize and remember those times when you were not a very good leader based on the above criteria. If you're anything like me, you can recall dozens of times you failed miserably and inflicted a lot of pain. Fortunately, the past is the past, and this isn't a pass/fail exam on leadership. Becoming who God intends us to be is a lifelong process. Just as I don't expect my sons to behave like mature adults while in their teens or early twenties, God doesn't expect us to be superb leaders right out of the gate. We grow into it through successes, failures, and challenges.

But it's critical in the process to be self-aware, consistently and honestly reflecting on where we are in the journey. We all have growth areas and issues that tend to be toxic. Ignoring them and hoping they go away is not the best strategy. Implementing management policies and hiring outside consultants won't fix our problems and make our businesses healthy if we aren't willing to be honest about our own health.

In the home, imposing more discipline and sending our kids to counseling won't make our families healthier if we're not willing to recognize our own internal dysfunction as parents.

As Friedman discovered, "I began to realize that before any technique or data could be effective, leaders had to be willing to face their own selves."[13]

So how *do* we face ourselves? It may be difficult looking in the mirror to examine where we fall short. And it may not work because our minds are great at making excuses for ourselves and twisting the facts. As alluded to earlier, we need others to give us honest feedback.

One of the many blessings and curses of marriage is being each other's mirror. If it's a healthy marriage, there's nothing like being loved unconditionally while having your flaws pointed out. If it's not healthy, things can get ugly real fast. But as leaders, it's imperative we accept criticism with humility and grace, because the consequences are too great if we don't. It's horrible to realize we may be daily inflicting pain on others just by being our sweet, little ol' selves and not having a clue. So here are some suggestions:

1. *Seek honest feedback from your staff and family.* This can be especially challenging, because if they're afraid of you, they're *not* going to give you an honest answer. Or they may really love you and won't want to hurt your feelings. If so, move on to #2.

2. *Have your entire staff take a Company Assessment Survey.* Ask questions about their job satisfaction, values, and the culture. Do they feel valued and respected? Is there a sense of purpose in their role? Their answers will reflect how you're doing as a leader. Don't take negative feedback defensively, but look at it as constructive. And make sure they understand their answers will be anonymous and can't be traced back to them. Otherwise, you're back to the problem above in #1.

3. *Measure your own anxiety levels.* It's one thing to be busy, but quite another to be anxious. Your anxiety is like the canary in the coal mine. It's the early warning signal that

something's not right. Listen to it, talk things over with a spouse or friend, and get to the bottom of it. Believe me, if you're anxious, everyone knows it, so you better face it rather than trying to hide it or deny it exists.

4. *Take the time to cultivate your interior life.* Read, pray, take walks, journal, attend a fellowship, have a weekly or monthly support group where you can openly share your dreams, hurts, and struggles. We're all in this together.

WHEN YOU *DO* LEAD . . . WE SUFFER

I'll end this chapter with an ironic twist on how it began.

If you're a business owner, or in any position with lots of responsibility, you know firsthand how hard it can be. You wear many hats, you never take a day off mentally, and you're on call 24-7, always worrying about what can and will go wrong, and you feel the weight of the world on your shoulders, as your employees and customers depend on you.

There are times I've worked twenty-hour days, suffered through migraines, been on the verge of emotional collapse and divorce, and simply felt I couldn't do this anymore. When my shop manager told me they all suffer when I don't lead, it wasn't the first time I withdrew into my cocoon to hide. I had been cycling through burnout for over twenty years.

The twist came about three years ago, when my body told me I'd had enough, as I came down with some illnesses that were a direct result of stress—of simply doing life too fast and hard.

Without being overly dramatic, I was faced with a decision, or perhaps an ultimatum: either radically change how I worked and lived, or face the consequences. That second way didn't hold much promise for a long life, or even a short and productive one. Either drastically rest, or my symptoms could easily morph into a stroke, heart attack, or who knows what. My body was shutting down to the extent that, no matter how hard I tried, I couldn't work more than a six-hour day.

So I held a company meeting and explained to everyone the doctor's prescription, that I needed a tremendous amount of rest. It would be best if I took off for six months. As a business owner, you can imagine how that was not an option. I explained how dire my health was and that if I didn't at least cut back substantially, I might have to sell the company. Even if I did rest, cut back my hours at the shop, and do everything perfectly, my recovery would take at least a year.

Well, I did cut back—but I did a lot of *other* things wrong, and my recovery actually took three years. I had a lot of time to think, pray, read, and reflect, but not because I wanted to. The irony was that when I led less, the company did better.

Friedman would say I was *over-functioning*. Others would say I was a control freak, which honestly, I don't believe I was. Instead, a better way to describe me would be as an enabler. If it was possible to care too much, I did. I cared too much about people, the jobs, the problems and issues that arose, and how people did or did not get along. In some unhealthy ways, people became *too* dependent on me as a leader. I spent so much time putting out fires, I continually burned myself out. I was continuously anxious and worried.

However, by being forced to cut back and be absent, it drew others into solving more of their own problems. Other leaders had to rise up, a number of employees moved on, new staff were hired, and the company went through a period of upheaval and chaos. I wasn't in shape to jump in and fix things, and we all wondered what the future held.

Some of our staff created a survey to get everyone's opinion. The results came in that, although the majority of the staff loved working at Edgerton Gear, there were a number of serious issues that needed to be addressed. In desperation, I reached out to a number of business associates, such as our banker, lawyer, and accountant. It was the owner of our HR firm who came back with a suggestion of reorganizing the leadership staff and coaching me to be a different kind of leader. Although I thought I was doing pretty well in regard to all the things discussed above, my next growth step was to be a better leader by leading less, not more.

In essence, I'm learning that when I lead too much, people suffer. When I lead too little, people also suffer.

The point is that I'm not a perfect leader, but God is in the process of helping me be the type of leader He desires. When I read Jesus' teaching, I see and hear Him telling me to be a servant: "So you want first place? Then take the last place. Be the servant of all" (Mark 9:35 MSG). That doesn't mean I'm a doormat. It does mean I need to be careful not to inflict pain but to bear it.

That's what non-anxious, self-aware, focused, committed leaders do.

10

Community and Culture

As I stood over his grave, I wasn't sure where to begin. I'd never met the man, but I knew his middle-aged, former military drill sergeant son needed to talk to him. The emotional wounds ran deep from his teenage years, when he had slowly watched his father die of a terminal illness, while his mother was out having an affair.

Now, as an adult almost forty years later, he was one of my key leaders in the shop, but the pain of the past, and the recent death of his second wife, often engulfed him to the point where he could hardly function. He needed his dad, as there were conversations they never had when he was a rebellious, angry, hurting teenager.

So now, as we together stood over his father's grave, I had offered to accompany him and get the conversation with his father started. I awkwardly introduced myself, as I spoke to the headstone and said I know he must be very proud of the man standing beside me. I then left the two alone and walked back to the car.

When I glanced back, he was on his hands and knees, his entire body heaving with sobs. Healing had begun.

THE BIG PICTURE

If you've stayed with me so far in this book, chances are you're either somewhat familiar or even very familiar with some of the Christian ideas I've used up to this point. But if the Christian concepts and words I've used are new territory for you, then you may find this next section especially foreign. Some explanation might be helpful. Bear with me; this actually does relate to the workplace.

Christian theologians have spent centuries studying the Bible to make sense of what God has done and is doing, as well as to predict what He plans to do. The storyline is this: a loving God created this world for the sheer joy of wanting to have others to whom He could give love, and from whom He could receive it.

However, it all went horribly wrong, as the human race screwed up and began to feel that as people, they didn't need God. Because we all went our own way, things predictably got even worse for us, and worse, and worse. We found ourselves killing each other, destroying the planet, and, frankly, making a mess of things.

However, God never gave up on us and had a strategy for wooing us back to Himself, simply because He loved us as a good parent would. He decided to pick a specific person (Abraham), and through him to begin a nation, to know Him in a special way. He hoped Abraham and his descendants would become a nation of priests to help other tribes and nations reconnect with the Creator.

However, this didn't go well either, as there were more wars, incest, hatred, greed, and a propensity to self-destruct. The nation that God originally chose was eventually conquered and essentially became a people without a country.

After several hundred years of seeming silence from heaven, with things on our planet arguably getting worse rather than better, God again intervened and His Son came in the flesh in the person of Jesus.

This was the plan all along—to show righteousness at its best against a backdrop of human failure at its worst. After we gave ruling the planet and our lives our best shot through power and intimidation, Jesus came, showing a radically contrary way of love, humility, and service. Of course, this threatened the powers that be, and Jesus was put to death. However, God's ace in the hole was bringing Jesus back to life, showing that evil had no power or hold on Him. He promised to return someday to set things right but in the meantime sent a Helper (His Spirit) to guide us to live accordingly.

That's a capsule summary of Christian theology. Personally, I think it's an extraordinarily brilliant plan, and does require a measure of faith. Sci-fi alien movies over the years have helped me see how this could all be true. Not that God is an alien; but then again, He is. We obviously need some outside help to figure out how to get along on this planet and not blow it to smithereens.

The Christian worldview makes more sense to me than any other I've looked at. I know there are lots of holes in my explanation, and some folks will pick it all apart. However, this isn't a thorough, careful treatise on Christian theology. I just wanted to give a little context for what theologians have come up with to describe what Jesus' role has been, is, and will be, which I'll now attempt to relate to how our faith in Jesus relates to our role in business.

As we discussed in the prior chapter, as leaders, we play a powerful role, specifically as it relates to the culture and sense of community in our workplaces. Like it or not, we're the ones responsible for creating the culture, which essentially dictates the values, traditions, beliefs, rules, assumptions, and dynamics of re-lating. Edgar Schein, in *Organizational Culture and Leadership,* stresses that leadership and understanding the culture in which leaders lead go hand in hand. Understanding how a culture is formed or changed is key to influencing and leading those within any organization:

> Cultures basically spring from three sources: (1) the beliefs, values, and assumptions of founders of organiza-tions; (2) the learning experiences of group members as their organization evolves; and (3) new beliefs, values, and assumptions brought in by new members and leaders.[1]

Therefore, as founders, owners, and/or leaders in our work-places, it's critical that we have a clear understanding of who we are, because as I've stated several times, our workplaces are exten-sions of ourselves. What we believe, what we value, how we relate to others, and even our personality quirks will shape and form the culture we're leading.

Our worldview and values become part of our workplace's DNA. Relating back to the previous chapter on leadership, it becomes obvious how our own personal health (emotional and spiritual) is so important. If we're toxic and dysfunctional, so will our workplaces be. If we're *well-differentiated* (Friedman), with a clear sense of our values and goals, have a healthy dose of humility and an unwavering commitment to the success of the organization (Collins and Level 5 leaders), the culture we create will flourish, as will our workplace.

So, with all this in mind, the questions I always ask are: "What culture am I to foster? What values and traditions will we hold dear? What kind of environment will allow our staff to thrive?" We're not a Google—a super wealthy tech company that feels more like a college campus, with video games, full service cafés, fitness centers, free bars, and fun slides. We're a machine shop.

> **As God's vessels of true inner goodness, leaders create and cultivate a kingdom culture.**

Going back to Van Duzer, how can I create meaningful employment, and what does that look like? It would be fun (and expensive) to keep up with the newest trends to make the workplace fun, but being a kingdom company runs deeper than just having fun. Rather than trying to keep up with what motivates millennials, Generations X and Y, baby boomers, and every other subgroup, I prefer to base our shop culture on what God intended culture and community to be. He's been at this a lot longer than any social scientist or human resource department. My Christian worldview tells me that God was not only the original creator of culture and community, but he is *still* actively at work shaping culture through us, if we allow him to.

A daily question I have to ask myself is, am I a willing participant of His work in my workplace? It has been my experience that most people haven't been taught or encouraged to think this way. This next section may be especially challenging if you're looking at the workplace through a Western mindset. In the United States, we like to think of leaders as *rugged individualists*, kings of their own little kingdoms, and masters of their destinies, where religion and faith have no place.

By now you can predict that I'm about to argue just the opposite. Jesus of Nazareth's teaching and the actual, real person of Jesus is perhaps never more relevant than in our businesses. Just hear me out.

JESUS AS PROPHET, PRIEST, AND KING

A theologian's job is to make sense of the cosmic drama I summarized above. Well-known symbols or images are often used to convey these ideas, just as we do in our everyday language. For example, we use terms like "Captains of Industry," "King of the Road," and "Knights in Shining Armor."

Theologians and all communicators do the same thing. So, if God does indeed care for the world, and Jesus is God in the flesh, what are some useful images we can relate to in order to understand how Jesus is accomplishing His mission? He definitely is in a position of power and authority, has been incredibly influential with His teaching, and philosophically has brought insightful ideas. We might use words like Master, President, Prime Minister, Lord, General Manager, CEO, Professor, or Captain to describe His role.

Since Jesus is connected to the deep traditions of the Judeo-Christian culture, theologians often draw deeply on the Old and New Testaments of the Bible for words and images that are familiar to that culture. Over the years, three of the words used to describe Jesus in both the New and Old Testaments are prophet, priest, and king.

Stevens's discussion on these three categories of leaders is especially helpful as an overview. Citing the Old Testament verse found in Jeremiah 8:1 and the reference to kings, prophets, and priests, he states,

> These three offices were leaders representing the people as a whole to God and representing God to the people— mediators and bridge builders. They were also mediating points of connection between God and the world . . . Israel needed all three. The priests ministered to the personal and spiritual needs; the prophets to the public and social needs, and the king to the organizational and political needs.[2]

In other words, God's intent was to create a community with a distinct culture that showed the world what it would be like for an entire group of people to be in constant communion, or relationship, with their Creator in a very healthy, everyday sort of way, not just on Sunday. As in our workplaces and in our communities, leaders are needed to encourage, promote, and demonstrate that culture on a consistent basis. In the Judeo-Christian tradition, the primary leaders who shaped their culture were prophets, priests, and kings.

Theologians have argued that Jesus has fulfilled these three offices, and if we're to take His mission seriously as His followers, we're extensions of Him. In other words, we're the ongoing expression of Jesus' ministry on earth. So how does this apply to a gear shop or any other business? Stevens again expands our view of ministry in the marketplace:

> What do prophets do? Their work is discerning, communicating, exposing, seeing that justice is done, revealing outcomes. . . .
>
> What do priests do? Their work is bridge building, mediating, expressing meaning, evoking faith, blessing, bringing grace. . . .
>
> What do kings do? King work is ruling, organizing, planning, providing, nurturing, integrating, settling arguments, solving problems, co-coordinating, expediting, consummating—again ways that God's people serve in so-called secular occupations, in church and in the home.[3]

When I came back to the shop in 1992, the late Pete Hammond (of InterVarsity Christian Fellowship) and Paul Stevens advised me that as I entered back into the family business, I should simply try and listen and discern what God has been doing. They wanted me to think of Edgerton Gear as God's business, and to know that He was more concerned about it than I was.

There were lots of problems. In essence, they were God's problems. What was He doing about them, and how could I join in His work? When I apply the grid of prophet, priest, and king, our gear shop is no longer about cutting oil, steel turnings, and the earthiness of blue-collar machinists. It now takes on a royal, ethereal quality, as it's transformed into a palace where God, the King, is at work. Let's take a closer look at these three offices and consider what they might look like in your workplace, with you in the role of facilitating God's work.

JESUS AS PROPHET IN THE WORKPLACE

When we think of a prophet, an image often comes to mind of a white-haired old guy in a robe with a long beard, kind of like the wizard Gandalf in *Lord of the Rings*. I don't have any idea if that's what they looked like in biblical times, but prophets and prophetesses (yes, there were women prophets) played a pretty significant role in the community. They were God's spokespersons, proclaiming His heart and intentions for His people.

In the Old Testament, individuals such as Moses, Isaiah, Jeremiah, Deborah, and Joel act as God's mouthpiece. In the New Testament, after Jesus leaves and sends the promised Helper (the Holy Spirit) on the day we now call Pentecost, all believers are now to partake in Jesus' prophetic ministry. In a machine shop full of blue collar machinists who rarely, if ever, go to church, how can Jesus fulfill His prophetic work through us?

Blue-collar folks are often overlooked in local churches. I affectionately refer to some of my staff as "the Harley riding, beer-drinking crowd." They rarely step foot in a church building, except for either weddings or funerals. Their perception of religion often comes through the media who often depict people of faith in a less-than-favorable light.

As in any workplace, ours has people with a wide range of spiritual backgrounds, and I don't want to offend or alienate anyone by forcing my spiritual beliefs on them. At the same time, I believe it's my responsibility to give them glimpses of the kingdom as we work together to make the best gears possible.

If a prophetic ministry entails showing God to man, then God's values, morals, and sense of purpose should be evident. In an industry notorious for alcoholism, owner-employee class conflict, and relational dysfunction, a culture of trust, dignity, and excellence stands in stark contrast to what most employees have experienced in their lives.

As one of my staff, who helped get his brother a job in our shop, just told recently me, "It's about time he's part of something bigger," meaning our shop provides a sense of purpose that is making a difference in the world.

Think back to how we defined *righteousness*. God's true inner goodness should be reflected through the workplace culture we lead. As we reflect God's values, morals, and standards, we're fulfilling the prophetic role of showing God to man. The three-legged stool of quality, value and, service is a reflection of God's character. The Golden Rule of treating others as we would want to be treated is God's instruction for how we should relate to one another.

> **Prophetic work in business is discerning, communicating, exposing, seeing that justice is done, and revealing outcomes.**

Here's a small yet practical example. A machine shop provides daily opportunities to demonstrate grace. As people, we all screw up. However, when a machinist screws up, it could easily cost thousands of dollars. Our employees have often told me that when they do something dumb that scraps out a very costly part, they would prefer me yelling and swearing at them, telling them how stupid they are, like other bosses, or perhaps like their parents.

My dad often told the story of when he worked for his stepfather in a gear shop in Chicago. Grandpa Joe, as I knew him, was a hard taskmaster of a man to work for. Dad would explain that if you made a mistake on a lathe and scrapped the part, Grandpa Joe would fly into a rage, slamming a file down so hard on the lathe that the file would snap in two. He'd then take the part and hang it over your machine as a humiliating reminder not to screw up again.

However, in our shop, we usually empathize with how bad they feel. We discuss how and why it happened to make sure we learn from the mistake, and simply start over. As much as possible, we teach how important it is to treat each other with compassion and understanding. Although there are times where discipline is warranted, it's important to balance truth with grace.

JESUS AS PRIEST IN THE WORKPLACE

A priest cares for the needs of the community. If your workplace is large enough to have a human resource department, you might assume that's their job—to care for the needs of the community. However, such caring runs much deeper than policies, procedures, and benefits. It's also how we can help care for the world, our communities, our customers, vendors, and each other. When leaders create a positive culture, they model and teach everyone how to care for each other.

So in the case of the world, I think of making gears as an act of *worship*.

It's not so farfetched. Our gears touch the lives of literally millions, if not billions, as they go into every conceivable kind of equipment that makes it possible for our world to have computers, cellphones, food, clothing, books, magazines, soda cans, canned goods, toilet paper, mining equipment, batteries, construction and farm equipment. Making gears is a form of intercession. As we lift up the needs of the world to God, He responds through us by making gears that run the equipment to produce products that enrich lives everywhere.

On a community level, our businesses can be like an army of priests throughout the community, as our staff live their daily lives and become aware of needs. We encourage our staff to be involved in the schools and community events and needs by paying them to "volunteer" where needed. Each employee is allotted up to twenty hours per year to chaperone their children's field trips, assist nonprofit organizations, and/or to help others in need.

> **Priestly work in the workplace is bridge building, mediating, expressing meaning, evoking faith, blessing, and bringing peace.**

On a company level, I have come to understand that many of my employees need a priest. But our "priests" come in the form of compassionate, shop floor leaders who model the Golden Rule of treating others as you want to be treated. It's always a challenging role, as people will be people and get caught up in rumors, slander, and quick judgments of each other. We all have good days and bad days, and we get moody, defensive, territorial, insecure, and stressed. How do we as a community handle failure, injustice, selfishness, pride, and being hurtful toward one another? Living and working for fifty hours a week or more in this small community of a gear shop doesn't provide a lot places to hide. All our wounds, scars, and shortcomings eventually become public, but so does God's grace, healing, and forgiveness.

We're continually learning how to get along, tolerate, and even appreciate our differences.

On a very practical level, priestly service to our staff plays a big role in compensation and benefits. We need to pay a living wage, provide adequate time off for personal matters and vacation, as well as seeing to health needs. In the United States, one of the great challenges for small businesses is health care. With costs spiraling out of control, it's increasingly difficult for small companies to absorb medical insurance costs. Twenty-five years ago, we could afford to pay 100 percent of the medical insurance premiums for our staff. Today we're struggling to pay 60 percent, with our staff paying the balance. The deductibles have increased to the point where no one can afford to get sick. There are no easy answers, and at the time of this writing, we're discussing together how to address the medical needs of everyone, while keeping the company profitable.

On a personal level, I've come to realize that for many of our staff, our company is their most important form of community, since this is where they spend the majority of their waking hours. Treating employees as objects or machines is inhumane and just plain wrong. We either create a culture that is life affirming, or we don't. For many that come from dysfunctional or fractured families, this is where they feel accepted, loved, and valued, and have a sense of purpose and identity. They often find emotional and even spiritual support. When their problems are larger, we help find professionals in counseling, health care, and financial coaching.

JESUS AS KING IN THE WORKPLACE

My American heritage doesn't have a favorable view of kings. In fact, my blue-collar world takes a rather dim view of politicians in general, let alone one who would claim to be a king. As a business owner, I've struggled to embrace my role as a leader since the blue-collar culture tends to be cynical and mistrusting of leaders in general. All of us here at Edgerton Gear, including me, have worked for bosses who lorded it over their staff and treated them as little more than machines. Matthew Crawford, in his discussion on the value of work, speaks about "the degradation of blue-collar work,"[4] as the industrial revolution sought to maximize productivity and profits at the expense of the dignity of the laborer. Craftsmanship had to make room for the assembly line, where managers sought to hoard knowledge and make tasks as simple and routine as possible. Crawford quotes one of Henry Ford's biographers, "So great was labor's distaste for the new machine system that toward the close of 1913 every time the company wanted to add 100 men to its factory personnel, it was necessary to hire 963. . . . Evidently, the new system provoked natural revulsion."[5] Machinists don't like being treated like machines. So how does one contextualize the notion of kingship in a gear shop if we intuitively distrust leaders?

On one level, Jesus working through me means constantly exercising justice in the community and in our industry. I'm called to serve through leadership, to be fair and just in business, to settle disputes among our employees, to offer a fair wage and share in our profits. By treating our customers with respect and fairness, we keep greed in check among our competitors and set the standard for service. There are times, as a business owner, I can speak on behalf of the poor and leverage resources for the disenfranchised.

On another level, I'm called to help create a peaceful community by modeling and empowering others to create a healthy sense of family. In a broken world, our staff is not immune to personal tragedies such as death, car accidents, mental illness, addiction, divorce, and bankruptcy. Edgerton Gear can be a refuge of healing, forgiveness, and grace. It's painful to watch their personal lives unravel. And yet, I've been told numerous times

As God's princes and princesses, our work is ruling, organizing, planning, providing, nurturing, integrating, settling arguments, solving problems, co-coordinating, expediting, and consummating.

over the years by different staff that they wouldn't know where they would be if not for Edgerton Gear, as we have helped carry their burdens.

Last, Jesus as King means protection and provision, both physically and spiritually. Daily, I'm called to lift up this company and its people in prayer, sometimes sensing that evil is trying to devour and destroy them. On occasion, I have been prompted or asked to pray with our employees, to wrestle with them in their addictions, and to pronounce blessings and renounce curses. As our staff has matured, we see numerous examples of coworkers caring and defending each other from abusive customers and vendors. One of our employees confronted a customer's pick-up driver who was sexually harassing our shipping clerk. We often see staff become a support network for each other, helping in and outside of work with personal issues, hobbies, and home projects.

We daily see God's provision. Customer orders consistently come at just the right time, often more orders than we can seemingly handle. Even during past recessions, though we could have maximized profits by reducing staff, we have never laid anyone off, as we all chose to make and work less for the sake of keeping the community together.

Customers and suppliers often marvel that we work only one shift. They often see our expensive equipment and wonder how we can afford to let it sit idle fourteen hours a day. However, many of us have worked in shops with two or more shifts, and it's rarely pleasant, as the sense of community is compromised. We've been fortunate to be able to stay with one shift, but it's also been a conscious choice to manage our workload and turn down potential customers if they're not a good match for our culture. As "kings," we're called by God to manage our businesses, not just to maximize profit but to strive to do what's best for everyone. Sometimes, profit doesn't come first.

YOUR CONGREGATION

I'm fully aware that using the words *prophet*, *priest*, and *king* might be a bit strange and even foreign to describe our roles as leaders who want the kingdom of God to be present in our workplaces. A more contemporary word for those from a Protestant tradition might be *pastor*. Even this word has roots in agriculture and animal husbandry in the context of caring for sheep. Many of us are familiar with referring to a pastor of a church congregation as also a shepherd, meaning those of us are being "shepherded" are the sheep. Jesus even told His disciple Peter that if he really loved

Jesus, he should "feed my sheep" (John 21:17). Many Protestant and Catholic churches use this passage to justify the role of paid, professional pastors and priests in organized church congregations.

Of course, I'll probably offend someone again for saying this, but this passage doesn't support that argument at all; in fact, there are only a few passages in all of the New Testament that mention ministers being compensated for their work. I would argue this is the exception rather than the rule, and hardly supports the case for a separate or elite class of professional, paid ministers and clergy we have today. I realize we live in a different time and place from the New Testament world, but we must be careful in thinking that to minister, in other words *to serve*, should be left to the religious professionals. The point is we *all* have a role to play in serving others. But I digress and that is not my main point.

I simply argue that when Jesus says "feed my sheep" to Peter, the writer of the gospel of John is making the case that if we're truly followers of Jesus and lovers of God, if we're in a position of leadership or authority, our first responsibility is to love and care for those whom we're leading and serving. As an aging man, decades removed from Jesus' life on earth, John reflects on his time with Jesus and writes several letters to explain what following Jesus means.

> This is how we know what love is: Jesus Christ laid down his life for us. And we ought to lay down our lives for our brothers and sisters. If anyone has material possessions and sees a brother or sister in need but has no pity on them, how can the love of God be in that person? Dear children, let us not love with words or speech but with actions and in truth. (1 John 3:16–18)

Over the years, I've come to think of our company as a congregation. We're a varied and diverse group of people, working in unison to achieve a collective goal of providing the best gears possible for our customers' needs. Remembering that two of everyone's greatest needs are purpose and relationships, we constantly strive to create an environment that provides both.

In our workplaces, we have infinite opportunities to love people on a daily basis. But as John says above, it's not just words or speech but with action; it's in how we create, define, and defend a life-giving culture; it's how we compensate our staff, serve our customers, and interact with our suppliers. Without even realizing it, as leaders in our organizations, we have more influence among our staff than many, if not most, pastors and priests do in their congregations. Since blue-collar machinists would be offended if I referred to them as sheep, I simply ask, are we feeding, nurturing, encouraging, empowering, affirming, and loving them through our actions?

11

Betrayal and Failure

"Honey, it's your dad."

I knew immediately something was up, as my wife handed me the phone. Dad hardly ever called me, especially in the evening after dinner. Besides, what couldn't wait until tomorrow when I would see him at work?

"We have a problem," he began. My stomach lurched. He was a suck-it-up, tough, understated, old-school guy, so if he said we had a problem, it must be a doozy. He then explained he had just discovered our assistant manager had been secretly setting up his own gear shop and lying through his teeth for the past six months. Right under our noses, he was making sweetheart deals with our customers and vendors to siphon away business from Edgerton Gear.

He had been my dad's right-hand man in the eight years I had been absent, and he had been my confidant as I tried to bring a new level of health and hope to the shop over the past eighteen months. How deep did this plot go? How many other employees were involved? We would soon find out the conspiracy was deeper and more widespread than we could imagine. Would the business survive?

The world is broken. People are broken. I know that, yet I'm surprised by this simple fact every day. You'd think by now that I would expect and embrace how broken this world is, especially since most of my career has been spent fixing broken things by making new gears to replace broken ones. Our business depends and even thrives on the fact that things wear out, that people screw up, and that things break. So why am I continually surprised, frustrated, and disappointed at how broken people are? As we say in the shop, making gears is easy. It's working with people that's the hard part.

Today, as I write this, it's the day after the Las Vegas massacre where a retired accountant plotted to unleash an incomprehensibly savage attack on concertgoers, where in the end, fifty-eight people were killed and over five hundred were wounded. One more brutal act of terror in a growing list over the past few years.

Closer to home, a wonderful, caring doctor who was a dear neighbor lost a short battle with lymphoma. His sister called today to ask if we could help at his funeral.

A friend of a friend's father committed suicide today.

My mother will have knee replacement in two weeks, as her body, like all of ours, continues to wear out.

My mother-in-law died this summer.

A wonderful coworker at the shop recently had a major stroke.

A dear friend is facing divorce after twenty-two years of marriage and three sons.

I can hardly stand to watch the news, read the paper, or even simply answer my own phone, as pain surrounds us on all sides. The world is broken.

A great deal of our human experience and a great deal of our daily work is about dealing with brokenness. Judeo-Christian theology teaches us about the fall—that moment in time when Adam and Eve decided they didn't need God—and things haven't been the same since. Whether you believe it was an actual event or a mythological story, the facts are pretty clear. Humankind is extremely messed up, and our capacity for self-destruction and harming each other is stunning.

And I don't have to watch the news to know this is true. I just have to get up and go to work. Betrayal, failure, and cutthroat competition are daily challenges we face. They remind me just why Jesus' pronouncement of God's kingdom set the world on its ear two thousand years ago and why we so desperately need God's kingdom to break into our workplaces today. This chapter attempts to shine some light on the darker side of the workplace that is far from unicorns and rainbows. Business is often gutwrenchingly painful. The marketplace will be cruel. People will let us down and betray us. We will fail. The world and all of us included are broken.

ANATOMY OF A BETRAYAL

When I came back to the family business almost three decades ago, I recognized it as one of the most hurtful places I knew. My sister was being treated badly. The staff was divided into warring factions, and everyone seemed to be grasping for their "rights," while displaying a level of cruelty far worse than what one might see on the playground.

In the midst of all the brokenness, I had to know the answer to one thing: could the God of the Bible and Jesus of Nazareth fix any of it, even in a Midwest, family machine shop? Was the kingdom of God relevant at all, or was it just some theological mumbo jumbo? My world was busted and I needed to know if there was any hope.

Coming back to the family business was a grand experiment to see what would happen if we brought kingdom values and faith into a dirty and dark factory. I had a plan, a theological education, mentors who believed in me, and the willingness of my parents to try to salvage the future of the business they started with blood, sweat, and tears. Without going into too many details, I'll repeat my earlier summary that the first two years were hellacious—and then things got worse. My little corner of the world was not just broken, it was coming apart at the seams.

It was during that time we discovered one of our vendors was helping some of our employees start a new gear shop to compete with Edgerton Gear. I was blindsided. I had listened to their complaints and frustrations, shared my heart and vision for the company, and sought their advice and support. I mistakenly believed they were 100 percent on board and excited about our future.

Little did I realize how wrong I was. They had kept quiet about it all, playing me to buy time to get their own shop started. They accessed our computer records and sent out letters to our customers promoting their new business. It was especially painful for my dad. He felt betrayed and was reminded of them every day as he drove past their new shop to and from work.

We desperately wanted revenge. We wanted them to suffer. We wanted them to fail miserably. I saw how deeply they hurt my father and I hated them for it. God's kingdom in a machine shop? Ha! As the months slowly passed, the taste of despair and bitterness was always on my tongue. What would Jesus say in these moments? Did He have any clue how hard this was?

Looking back, although those were defining and painful years, what we experienced really wasn't too uncommon in the business world. I'm sure you have your own stories, some much worse than mine. What carried me more than anything during the dark years was the simple realization that Jesus understood betrayal more than anyone who ever lived—and yet He was without sin.

Of course, you could argue that He had divine powers, being the Son of God and all, and it was easier for Him than for us mere mortals. If you believe that for even a second, go back and read your Bible. In the gospel of Luke, we read that Jesus was in so much emotional anguish after being betrayed by Judas and knowing He'd soon be tortured and killed, that He sweated blood. I always thought this was just a figure of speech, but it's actually a rare medical condition called hematidrosis, in which you literally sweat blood, supposedly resulting from extreme stress or fear.

The way forward was horrific. Alone, secluded, and under the night sky, His prayer was not a pious, stoic ritual but was a cry with every ounce of His being.

> "Father, remove this cup from me. But please, not what I want. What do *you* want?" At once an angel from heaven was at his side, strengthening him. He prayed on all the harder. Sweat, wrung from him like drops of blood, poured off his face. (Luke 22:42–44 MSG)

It's moments of pain and betrayal that expose our depth (or lack thereof) of commitment to the kingdom of God. For God's kingdom and His righteousness, His true goodness, is not just a higher standard of ethics and morality. It's a profoundly different way of seeing, thinking, and acting.

Just because I'm in pain and somebody did me wrong does not give me the right to fight back, to lash out and take revenge. On the contrary, in our pain, it's of the utmost importance that we stop and consider what course of action God would have us take rather than waste time and energy agonizing over why God would allow others to hurt us.

Hopefully I'm not being callous when I say this. It's natural and not unexpected for us to shake our fist at God when heinous crimes like mass shootings, rape, and incest are committed. We wonder how any of this could possibly be God's will. But I can say with the utmost confidence in God's love that these things are *never* in God's will. His desire for us to be in harmonious relationship with each other, our planet, and with Him is profoundly beyond our comprehension.

But love demands He give us all free will, and it's heart-wrenching to see how harmful and destructive we often choose to be. Yet the tremendous mystery and depth of God's love also causes Him to counteract the brokenness and messes of our choices and lives if we allow Him to. Somehow, some way, good will come of it—as the apostle Paul wrote to the Christians in Rome, who were undergoing persecution and execution, "We know that in all things God works for the good of those who love him, who have been called according to his purpose" (Rom. 8:28).

But having faith that things will work out for the good is more than passive belief and trying to think happy thoughts when your world is coming apart. At the funeral of our doctor neighbor this past week, as one of his heartbroken sons said in his eulogy, "As my father taught me, there's a big difference between *knowing* what's right and *doing* what's right."

This is where true inner goodness comes into play. It's where the kingdom of God takes its stand and says, "Enough!" It's where our responses to betrayal, malice, and evil are guided not by the degree of the crime, but by the depth of our faith in God's goodness and care for us.

Consider for a moment Joseph's story in Genesis we briefly touched on in chapter 8. I can't even begin to imagine what it would have been like to be thrown in a pit by my own brothers, then sold as a slave to a traveling caravan. My sisters and I had our fair share of pranks, but selling your sibling as a slave?

I often wondered what was going through young Joseph's mind as he sat in the pit. If not for brother Reuben, Joseph would have been killed and left to rot in the dry well. Instead, they agreed to just throw him in and what? Die a slow death of hunger and thirst? This is a brutal story.

I wonder if Joseph thought they were just pranking him and that at any moment, the joke would be over. But a caravan of traveling merchants showed up, and Joseph did indeed get out of the pit, only to discover that he was being sold as a slave. When did it hit him that this was real? How many times in the days, weeks, months, and years ahead did he think this was all a bad dream and his father would come and rescue him?

Obviously, we don't know the answers, but we do know how gut wrenching the reunion was decades later when his brothers came to Egypt begging for food during the devastating drought.

Had he dreamed of this day to exact revenge? We often focus

on the wonderful moment when he finally revealed his true identity to his brothers. But consider his inner turmoil in the preceding months, as he held one brother hostage. I think it shows that he never fully got over their crime against him, even as he rose to the second most powerful position in Egypt.

True inner goodness means our responses to betrayal, malice, and evil are guided not by the degree of the crime, but by the depth of our faith in God's goodness and care for us.

And yet, if we read carefully over Joseph's life, we read that the Lord was with him, and he prospered. We see a man who could be trusted always to do the right thing. Even as he was betrayed at least two more times, which resulted in an extended stay in prison, he didn't allow this to define him. He didn't wallow in self-pity and bitterness, though I'm sure it was far from easy.

As the years passed, his reputation grew as someone who could be trusted—as someone wise and discerning. Did his faith in God ever waver? If he was human, it had to. Did it keep him from doing what he knew to be right in whatever situation?

The evidence suggests otherwise.

LOVE FOR ENEMIES

Going back to the Sermon on the Mount in Matthew, Jesus says the following:

> "You have heard that it was said, 'Love your neighbor and hate your enemy.' But I tell you, love your enemies

and pray for those who persecute you, that you may be children of your Father in heaven. He causes his sun to rise on the evil and the good, and sends rain on the righteous and the unrighteous. If you love those who love you, what reward will you get? Are not even the tax collectors doing that? And if you greet only your own people, what are you doing more than others? Do not even pagans do that? Be perfect, therefore, as your heavenly Father is perfect." (Matt. 5:43–48)

Later in his letter to the Romans, the apostle Paul gives very specific instructions on how to handle evil:

Do not repay anyone evil for evil. Be careful to do what is right in the eyes of everyone. If it is possible, as far as it depends on you, live at peace with everyone. Do not take revenge, my dear friends, but leave room for God's wrath, for it is written: "It's mine to avenge; I'll repay," says the Lord. On the contrary: "If your enemy is hungry, feed him; if he is thirsty, give him something to drink. In doing this, you will heap burning coals on his head." Do not be overcome by evil, but overcome evil with good. (Rom. 12:17–21)

These are stories and words I've held on to for dear life in my years in business. The action of applying them is how we usher in the kingdom of God in our work and life.

In our litigious culture, where trial lawyers are waiting in the wings to sue someone so we can take monetary revenge for the wrongs done to us, God paints another picture of grace, forgiveness, and peace. Could we have sued the three employees who betrayed us? Sure, we could have tried. Would it have done any good? Probably not. In fact, in the upside-down world of God's kingdom, it turned out they did us a huge favor. Without the parting of ways with them and the vendor who helped them, we would not have needed to find an alternative gear material, which led us to start another business, which became the vehicle for some of Edgerton Gear's biggest customers to find us.

Not all acts of betrayal lead to prosperity and success. But they may, if God so wills it. Or they may not. It doesn't really matter, does it? What's really at stake is whether we will allow the crime to hurt us over and over and over by holding on to the bitterness and desire for revenge. As I'm sure Jesus had in mind when He taught on forgiveness, holding on to our anger is the gift that keeps on giving, and not in a good way. Let it go, let it go, let . . . it . . . go.

FAILURE? TO WHOM?

My youngest son called me today from college. He's in his third year of studies as a business major, and his second year as a resident assistant in the dorms. It's a great job that provides room and board while developing his leadership skills.

Today, he said he was dealing with one of his residents, who was having thoughts of suicide. He then commented on how quick his generation is to believe they're worthless and absolute failures.

I don't have any statistics to back this up, but he's probably correct. Most of us are personally familiar with the tragedy of a human being taking his or her own life. Many of us have even considered it ourselves. Again, I don't have statistics, but it seems it's far more common than it used to be. Or are we just more aware of it because of social media? Or is social media partially to blame, as young people have a medium to instantly compare themselves to everyone and anyone?

When an individual experiences an extreme sense of failure, the result is often losing the will and reason to live. I know this is a morbid way to start this section, but this phenomenon of "failure" is just that, a phenomenon that may or may not have anything to do with reality. But if we *perceive* ourselves as failures, the effect can be devastating.

But here is an odd question. When describing a human being, is there any such thing as being a failure? Of course, we all make mistakes, screw up, and often fall woefully short of our own and others'

Does God ever see us as failures?

expectations. But does any of that mean we're actually "failures"? Bear with me on this one before you put me in the camp of certain soccer parents, where there are no winners or losers and everyone gets a trophy.

In real life, sometimes we do win. Sometimes we lose. There are natural consequences to our choices and actions. In business, if our products are horrible, overpriced, and we don't serve our customers, I guarantee our business *will* fail. We may fail as parents, in marriage, or in how we handle finances, friendships, addictions. I have yet to meet anyone who doesn't feel like they have failed at something.

But again I ask, does this mean we're failures, especially in God's eyes? Perhaps the better question is: Do any of our failings in life mean we are beyond God's reach? How we answer this question can literally be a matter of life and death. To the degree that we perceive ourselves to be failures is, I believe, directly correlated to the degree of joy and love we experience in this life. And since our perception of ourselves is often faulty, I propose it's critical for us to see ourselves not as we *think* we are, so far down the path of failure, that we're beyond help and hope, but rather as a child of God who always welcomes us back with open and loving arms. The truth is what really matters.

Nowhere does God ever refer to a person as a failure. In fact, the worst I can come up with is when God is displeased with us because of how self-destructive we can be and hurtful towards others. He speaks through the prophets in the Old Testament and points out how rebellious and sinful we're. The word *sin* basically refers to "moral wrongdoing, injury, mischief, enmity, feud, guilt, crime, and offense against God."[1]

I don't want to speak for God, but it seems to me His anger comes out of His desperate love for us, similar to when we get angry at our kids for doing stupid stuff because we love them. We know stupid actions are going to have consequences, just like our sin is going to keep us from living a less than ideal life that God desires for us.

I think we all can agree with the apostle Paul when he says to the Christians in Rome that all have sinned and fallen short of God's glory, or in other words, not measured up to His perfection and majesty. I like Eugene Peterson's way of saying this: "We are utterly incapable of living the glorious lives God wills for us" (Rom. 3:23 MSG).

But this doesn't mean we're failures. On the contrary, Jesus' entire pronouncement of God's kingdom, that He invites us to join, is to recognize that we're God's dearly beloved, His special creation, fearfully and wonderfully made, no matter how much we *fail*. As hard as this may be to believe, our actions have little bearing on how much God loves us.

If you find this difficult to comprehend, think about your own perspective. If you have children, do you ever stop loving them when they screw up? One of the most dynamic elements of God's kingdom is that there simply are no failures, losers, outcasts, lowlifes, untouchables, or unloveables. In fact, God seems to especially show favor to those society despises and/or those who have come to believe themselves to be utterly worthless.

This is a profound truth we need to be constantly reminded of in the rough-and-tumble world of business. We won't survive very long if we're prone to self-pity and take our setbacks personally. If you're in the workplace long enough, you will undoubtedly experience failure on many levels.

You will fail your customers by delivering faulty products, not delivering on time, and not meeting their needs exactly as they

One of the most dynamic elements of God's kingdom is that there simply are no failures, losers, outcasts, lowlifes, untouchables, or unloveables.

want them met. You will fail your coworkers by taking your bad mood out on them, not being appreciative enough, and not meeting their needs exactly as they want them met. You will fail to charge enough and thus lose money on projects. You will overbid and thus fail to get the project in the first place. You will choose bad vendors, suppliers, and partners. You will hire people who disrupt your culture. You will choose poor leaders.

The opportunities to fail are endless on a daily basis. But this should never, ever mean you personally are a failure, beyond hope and help.

SO, WHAT DID WE LEARN?

The greatest benefit of failure is hopefully learning and growth. Nobody likes failure. It's painful, embarrassing, and can damage one's self-esteem and confidence. But we learn more from our failures than we do from our successes. I've often heard it said, "If you're not failing, you're not trying."

Machinists who are afraid to fail often don't make good machinists. You have to be willing to take a risk, be creative, see what works and doesn't work. It's how we learn. It's how *everyone* learns. As Henry Ford said, the "greatest thing in life is experience. Even mistakes have value."[2]

I think every person in the workplace in the history of the world can tell stories about their failures. In business, we perhaps have more opportunities for failure than most people because we're risk takers. It's in our DNA. We see challenges as opportunities. We often get bored with *what is* and look beyond to what *could be*. Oftentimes we're successful, sometimes wildly so. Many times, we experience crushing defeat and failure. It's the nature of business.

One of my biggest failures started fifteen years ago, and I'm still paying for it. Or, put another way, I'm still reaping the benefits of the lessons.

It all started when an engineer friend of mine started the conversation with, "Don't say no! Just hear me out." That should have been my first clue to kick his butt out the door.

He had redesigned an old machine with new technology and was convinced there was a huge need for it, and he needed a machine shop to build it. My initial instincts were to decline his offer, as we were a gear shop and this wasn't a gear. However, agreeing to think about it, I sought the counsel of my staff and everyone agreed it sounded like a great opportunity. I seriously prayed about it for several days, but there were no obvious reasons not to say yes.

However, something didn't feel right. I had this nagging sense that I was walking into a storm—and that I was *supposed* to. So, against my better judgment, I agreed. And thus, we started a ride into the abyss that we wouldn't get out of for over a decade.

My new partner told me the engineering was almost finished. What he didn't make clear at the time was that his idea of being "almost finished" wasn't even remotely close to my definition. Furthermore, he had an experienced salesman all lined up who was extremely confident the machines would sell so fast, our shop wouldn't be able to keep up. With just "a little" capital, this business venture was a sure thing, or at least as close to a sure thing as possible.

Well, you can probably guess the outcome, but you'd only be half right.

The salesman needed a salary, and my partner had a couple of engineering buddies we had to hire to help "finish things up." To make a long story short, the salesman sold only one machine in the first eighteen months, and the engineers billed us for *hundreds* of hours.

Before I knew what hit us, we were $300,000 in the hole with no strong sales prospects. We went into crisis mode. We fired the salesman and the engineers.

Things then went from bad to worse. One of the engineers had spent some time in our shop and had downloaded pirated software onto one of our computers. Suddenly, I was getting legal notices that stated we were in violation of licensing laws and we either had to pay tens of thousands of dollars in fines or be sued.

My partner then came to me and said he was being audited by the IRS and because of Edgerton Gear's affiliation with him, we would probably be included in his audit. It was revealed that he had a number of bad and shady business dealings. The reputation my parents worked so hard to build for Edgerton Gear was about to be dragged through the mud with him. If we were in crisis mode before, now it was a matter of triage to stop the bleeding and imminent death.

We needed to cut the cord with him and distance ourselves from each other as fast as possible. I offered to buy out his share of our partnership, which I did at a discount. However, this only added to our debt. So I had to finance the debt from my other two companies, which were fortunately profitable. I hired our lawyer to negotiate and settle with the software company.

The entire venture was, by far, the worst business decision I had ever made. Bankruptcy was considered, but only as a last resort. I was always taught to do whatever it takes to keep your word and pay your bills. Besides, my parents had spent a lifetime building a reputation of being trustworthy, responsible, and frugal, and I had no intention of screwing that up.

So we buckled down and turned one of our machinists into a part-time salesman. We continued to advertise on the internet, and slowly the inquiries came in. As we'd done at Edgerton Gear, we approached every potential client as another opportunity to serve someone rather than as just another potential sale. Within a year, we'd sold a few machines. Within five years, we sold a few more. A full fourteen years later, we finally broke even and made a little profit. In the short-term, we failed miserably. In the long-term, the business has been far from a success, unless you define success as breaking even after fifteen years!

As a tragic follow-up to this story, about two years after I bought out my partner, the bank came calling on him and said they could no longer give him any credit. They called in his note, and he went home and put a gun to his head.

Nobody had known how deep in debt he was, not even his wife. As with many people, his identity was directly connected to his success or failure in business. Unfortunately, he didn't grasp that, in God's eyes, his failed business dealings didn't exclude him from God's love and help.

The lessons learned are obvious. If it sounds too good to be true, it usually is. Don't get caught up in hype and expectations. Get facts and get them verified by third parties. Don't go into any partnership unless you know the other party *really* well, but even then, remember most partnerships don't work out in the long run. Slow and steady wins the race . . . hopefully.

The experience as a whole has made me a much better business person and helped me avoid many similar mistakes. It has definitely been a blow to my ego, but I can honestly say I don't know if I would have done anything differently because I needed to learn these lessons. Did I fail? Spectacularly! Did it make me a failure? Only if I had let it.

You see, here is where one of the most astounding yet profound mysteries of the kingdom impacts real life. And it all comes back to where we started with seeking God's kingdom and His righteousness, His true inner goodness.

IMPUTED RIGHTEOUSNESS

If we can agree the world is broken, and if we can also agree one of the greatest tragedies of our human existence is our sense of worthlessness, Jesus ushering in God's kingdom is the singular, most radical and important event in the history of the world.

It also is the number one reason why our workplaces have the potential to be the greatest vehicles to change the world today and why every follower of Jesus should consider how impactful their work can be.

Pretty bold statement, huh? But consider the following.

Pretty much every war, all poverty, all man-made ecological disasters, and most personal heartache and tragedies can be traced back to a sense of failure. Remember our earlier origins of failure being a deficiency or lacking thereof? Aren't all wars fought because one or both parties felt they were lacking in some way and wanted more, even if it meant taking what belonged to someone else? Isn't poverty the result of a number of deficiencies, such as a lack of education and resources, as well as deficiencies in quality relationships that provide access to the marketplace, along with the spiritual depravity of everyone involved?

Those who are in control of the marketplace often feel they lack enough and are therefore driven by the need to possess more, and thus prevent others from joining. Aren't man-made ecological disasters a result of perceived deficiencies of resources and wealth at others' expense, not realizing their need for more has ecological and environmental consequences?

Last, don't we all carry around a sense of deficiency, wondering whether we measure up, yearning for something more that we often can't identify?

When Jesus pronounced God's kingdom, He essentially said, "Enough of these lies, this greed, and your endless lust for more! What you all really want is peace, joy, and a sense of worth and belonging—to simply know you're loved. And I'm here to show you how to get there."

In a nutshell, we all have a deep-seated need to be *good*, for that is who God created us to be. To be *good*, is to be like God, for God is the very definition of goodness. He is love,

> **To be *good*, is to be like God, for God is the very definition of goodness.**

truth, hope, joy, compassion, courage, strength, trustworthiness, dependability, excellence, perfection, and kindness, all rolled into one.

He intended for us to be like him, as the writer of Genesis says: we were created *in His likeness.* Yet it all went horribly wrong, and we've been trying futilely to get back there ever since.

In His Sermon on the Mount, Jesus painted a picture for everyone of how life was meant to be lived and how we're to treat each other. His message deeply resonated with the masses, who were broken, hopeless, and oppressed, and He called them back to the life God intended. The obvious question—the elephant in the room—is "How? How do we get there when the world we live in is so far from this good life, this deep goodness, He spoke about?"

Jesus' response was as simple as it was earth-shattering. (Allow me to paraphrase.) "How do you get there? *Through Me.* Surrender how you think, act, breathe, eat, and live. Surrender your weak and pathetic attempts to be good to My sense of goodness. No longer seek your goodness, seek God's goodness because His is the *only* goodness that is actually true and good."

Now stay with me, because this is where being in business can get really exciting. If we go all the way back to Van Duzer's two purposes of business—(1) to provide goods and services for a community to allow it to survive and thrive and (2) to provide meaningful employment in terms of purpose and in the context of team, group, or entity of contributing members (that is, a business)—the sad reality is that the world is broken and everyone we interact with, such as employees, vendors, and customers, is broken as well. They carry around this deep yearning for goodness.

As followers of Jesus, we constantly strive for His kingdom and His goodness. We recognize that we're not and cannot be inherently good in how we conduct our lives and run our businesses. But Jesus offers *His righteousness*, His goodness to us. In big theological terms, He *imputes*, or transfers, His goodness onto us (Rom. 4:24). He deposits His fund of rightness into our morally bankrupt accounts.

So, as we operate day to day, as we seek God's kingdom and His true inner goodness, God lives His life through us. His goodness is given, or *imparted*, to us as we consciously make decisions throughout our day. As we seek Him through prayer, reflection, reading Scripture, and other writings, as well as getting counsel from others who are also seeking God, our thought processes and decision-making abilities begin to conform to how God thinks and wants things done.

Our actions then begin to be dictated by God's *righteousness*, by His goodness. His righteousness is not just a theological theory or word. Righteousness is goodness in action. And when this goodness begins to permeate every aspect of our work, surely the kingdom of God is at hand.

Our workplaces become beacons of light, goodness, hope, and belonging. Of course, we can choose not to be such beacons, such vessels of God's goodness. But why would we not?

As we seek God's kingdom and his true inner goodness, God lives his life through us.

In our final chapters, it's my hope you'll be inspired to discover your own walk of faith in the workplace and to explore the infinite ways you can be a vessel of God's kingdom.

12

Business as Love

We'd been up since two o'clock in the morning to catch an early flight to Honduras. We were anxious to get to the job site, to see the progress on the orphanage.

As the nine of us from Edgerton Gear climbed out of our vans, Carlos did not give us a jubilant greeting. Instead, he looked worried and perhaps even a little scared. "Daveed, we need to talk."

I asked him what was wrong, and he explained that the construction site had been vandalized. Electrical power lines were cut, tools were missing, and workers were quitting, as they feared for their lives. The worst part was that he knew who the culprits were; they were the area residents and neighbors.

I asked him why they would do such a thing. He said they were angry as they discovered this building was going to be an orphanage, not a medical center. They didn't want an orphanage in their neighborhood, but they did need a medical center.

"No entiendo (I don't understand)," I said. *"Why would they think this was going to be a medical center?"*

Carlos's response stunned me. "Because that's what we told them and the mayor to get this building lot for free. We're having a town meeting tonight. Could you come and talk to them before they become an angry mob?"

At the age of nineteen, I was a depressed, suicidal, binge-drinking mess. My mother once told me that at that time, my father didn't think I would ever amount to anything. Considering the current path I was on, I couldn't disagree. However, six months later, his opinion of me dramatically changed, to the point where he thought I could take over the business and easily double it. What happened to me in those six months that made people take notice? Without being overly mushy, in a single word: *love.*

I came to deeply believe that I was loved by someone much bigger than myself. In religious terms, I had a conversion experience. To this day, I can't understand or explain it, except to say that I became convinced beyond a shadow of a doubt that not only was there a God of the universe, but that He unconditionally and passionately loved me, even while I was a suicidal drunk. Love is a powerful force.

I refuse to get into arguments with people about the existence of God, the age of the universe, and any other science versus religion arguments. Personally, I think science and religion complement each other, if we can just get over our dogma and hang-ups. I also refuse to argue over whether my conversion was real or imagined. All I know is my life was radically changed and continues to be so. Love is a powerful force.

What's love got to do with business? I can speak only for myself: I'm in business because I'm loved and my response is to love others. It's as simple as that. When someone has been incredibly generous to us, hopefully our natural inclination is to be generous to others. God's love is like that for me. So, however possible, I want the totality of my life to be a response to the overwhelming love I experience from him.

Since the majority of my life is one of being a machinist and business owner, it logically follows that this is where my love finds expression in how I treat our staff, customers and vendors, and in the act of making a gear that serves humanity. I can think of no other entity or way to love and serve humanity so powerfully than through business. I'll even go so far as to argue that if everyone in business had this view, there would be no need for nonprofit organizations, because businesses would be truly seeing to the needs of their communities.

Idealistic, I know, but that's how my mind thinks. So, bear with me as we delve deeper.

DEFINITION OF PHILANTHROPY

It's interesting to break the word *philanthropy* into its two Greek roots. (Hey, even a crusty machinist can find words fascinating!) It's made up of the Greek words *phileo*, which refers to having or showing affection and *anthropos*, which refers to mankind. Put the two together, *phileo* + *anthropos*, and we have the word *philanthropy*, which means something like "the love of mankind."

One could argue that God is the ultimate definition of philanthropy, since the Bible tells us that God is love. Jesus therefore is the ultimate embodiment of philanthropy since He tells us there is no greater love than this: to lay down one's life for one's friends, which He did in an unimaginable way (John 15:13).

So when He tells us that the second greatest commandment is to love our neighbors as ourselves, He's instructing us to be philanthropic, to love mankind. Pretty straightforward, right? What's *not* straightforward is how we complicated it, screwed it up, and made a whole industry out of it.

Consider how the *Merriam-Webster* dictionary officially defines *philanthropy*:

> 1 : goodwill to fellow members of the human race *especially* : active effort to promote human welfare
> 2 a : an act or gift done or made for humanitarian purposes
>   b : an organization distributing or supported by funds set aside for humanitarian purposes[1]

Number 1 makes perfect sense. I'm even okay with number 2a, philanthropy as an act or a gift for humanitarian purposes—although it's starting to hint at being more grand and sophisticated than it needs to be.

Number 2b is where the hairs on the back of my neck start to stand up, and I get a little hot under the collar. This definition is "an organization distributing or supported by funds set aside for humanitarian purposes." It's no longer a personal act of loving other humans but is now an *organization*.

What's wrong with that, you say? Am I saying that organizations are bad? Businesses are organizations. Congregations are organizations. Nonprofit organizations that exist to help (that is, to love) humankind are obviously organizations. So, what's my problem with organizations?

My problem with organizations, when we talk about philanthropy, is simply this. Philanthropy was never meant to be big business. The sad fact in our modern world is that we have turned the simple act of loving our neighbor into a colossal industry that is fleecing well-intentioned people of *billions* of dollars. We have ruined local economies by dumping free stuff into developing countries in the name of *relief.*

Philanthropy has become such a huge industry that sometimes executives and officers are paid salaries comparable to hot-shot Wall Street types. I hesitate to list specific organizations, because you might be supporting one of them. But before you write another check, look the charity up on www.charitynavigator .org. It's not unusual to discover that a number of famous and well-known "nonprofit" charitable organizations are paying their CEOs and top executives well over $500,000 a year, and sometimes over $1,000,000.

When some of these "charities" come knocking on the door of our business, asking for a contribution, it's insulting to realize my $100 (or even $1,000) donation is hardly paying for some of these people's lunch! Our thirty-five-person shop, working together for an entire year, doesn't generate enough profit to pay for one yearly salary of some of these highly paid executives. Under no circumstances can you ever convince me that anyone should be paid this much to love humankind or to lead an organization to do so. It's insanity.

I get pretty wound up about this, because by simply giving money to a nonprofit organization, we may actually be doing more harm than good. A fascinating documentary, well worth your time, is *Poverty, Inc.* with the descriptive tagline "Fighting Poverty Is Big Business, but Who Profits the Most?"[2] It does a fabulous job of explaining how our good intentions can be so misguided. For example, a church in Texas decided to airlift thousands of eggs to a community in Africa. It sounds innocent enough, but by so doing, they put the local egg suppliers out of business. When the church stopped sending free eggs, there was no longer any place for the locals to buy eggs.

The more shocking stories show how little of our donation may get to its intended purpose, as it's eaten up by levels of bureaucracy where everyone gets a cut. The movie points out that free stuff may actually be contributing to ongoing poverty rather than alleviating it. It's stunning to hear members of some of the poorest nations on earth tell us to stop giving them free stuff, as its destroying their country.

What they *really* need and want is access to the marketplace, which is often dominated and manipulated to keep the poor dependent on big multinational corporations and governments.

My cynicism is not just from watching a movie or reading a book about the topic. I've experienced firsthand the corrupting power of money in the philanthropic world. As our company prospered, I sought numerous ways to give back. Our first negative experience happened when we attempted to open a foster home. The government regulation and difficulty of getting agencies to work together frustrated us to the point that we gave up.

We then attempted to be very generous to our local community assistance organizations. We still are, but the reality is that there's more government and community assistance available in our state than probably anywhere in the world. Unfortunately, we often foster dependence on welfare and handouts rather than finding creative ways to help people experience the dignity of providing for themselves.

Greed is not only a problem among the middle and upper classes. Too often, I've witnessed it just as much among the poor, as attitudes of entitlement become ingrained.

Some years ago, I felt a conviction to seek out those often referred to as the "poorest of the poor," meaning those who live in places in the world often beyond governmental assistance. I embarked on a nine-month research project and took seven trips to Central America to interview potential nonprofit organizations with whom we might form partnerships.

My cynical business mind didn't trust their websites or glossy newsletters. I needed to be on the ground, face to face, to see how efficiently they operated.

You'd think I'd done my due diligence when we partnered with a (supposedly) reputable organization in Honduras. After several trips to visit them, we even decided to send a work crew, consisting of ten of our staff, to help build an orphanage. On our crew's second trip, when we arrived, we were greeted by the nephew of the director. He pulled me aside and told me we had big trouble. The locals that lived near the soon-to-be orphanage were furious and intent on sabotaging the building project.

When I asked why, he responded that the neighbors thought they were getting a medical center, *not* an orphanage! As it turned out, the director told the city he'd build a medical center if they were given free land. There was a big ceremony, as the mayor dedicated the land.

But it was all a lie. When we confronted the director, an American, he flippantly said, "Who cares what they want? No one wants to give to a medical center. It's the kids who sell"— meaning that pictures of orphans bring in donations.

We also soon discovered that all the clothing, school

supplies, and other material donations we were bringing from the US to support one of his "orphanages" were not being given to children but were being sold. It turned out that the old, sweet grandma who ran the "orphanage" was actually the mother to a number of prostitutes, and the so-called orphans were actually the children of her daughters.

We obviously wanted no part in his lies and deceit, and I almost gave up. But I already had one more trip scheduled to visit another organization. Fortunately, that trip was a game changer, as we finally found a group of people who shared our vision of making a lasting impact among the poor by giving them education and hopefully the tools to break the cycle of poverty for their communities.

Over the next six years, I met dozens of other folks who recognized that the answer to poverty was not just giving away free stuff. I eventually became ill and needed to stop my travels, but the experiences were invaluable in shaping my evolving opinions of philanthropy. Consider the following.

The whole idea of philanthropy has been wrestled with for hundreds of years. A Jewish philosopher named Moses ben Maimon (Maimonides), who lived from 1135–1204, defined charity's eight degrees by ranking them. Even back then, people struggled with what was the best way to help those in need. What's especially interesting about Maimonides' list is that he takes into account our inner attitudes or postures when helping others.

Much like today, we can be harassed into feeling obliged to give, get credit for our good deeds, be anonymous, keep it just between us and God, or do the hard work of getting at the root of why the person is poor. As we go down his list, it gets more and more difficult, challenging our commitment, humility, and spiritual health:

1. A person gives, but only when asked by the poor.
2. A person gives, but is glum when giving.
3. A person gives cheerfully, but less than he should.
4. A person gives without being asked, but gives directly to the poor. Now the poor know who gave them help and the giver, too, knows whom he has benefited.
5. A person throws money into the house of someone who is poor. The poor person does not know to whom he is indebted, but the donor knows whom he has helped.
6. A person gives his donation in a certain place and then turns his back so that he does not know which of the poor he has helped, but the poor person knows to whom he is indebted.
7. A person gives anonymously to a fund for the poor. Here the poor does not know to whom he is indebted, and the donor does not know whom he has helped.

But the highest is this:

8. Money is given to prevent another from becoming poor, such as providing him with a job or by teaching him a trade or by setting him up in business so he will not be forced to the dreadful alternative of holding out his hand for charity. This is the highest step and the summit of charity's golden ladder.[3]

Quite frankly, I can relate to all eight of these, as I've tried to figure what's best. I've given just when asked; with a bad attitude, less than I probably should have; given and had the recipient feel indebted; tried to be anonymous, but then got resentful when I found the recipient wasn't as grateful as I thought they should be; given to someone else who distributes, so I don't know who is receiving; and given to a general fund of a nonprofit whose mission is to help those in need.

Quite honestly, *none* of these felt quite right. It's a wonderful privilege to be able to give money to help others, but there just seemed to be something missing. What I finally realized was that I have the means to do what Maimonides describes as the ultimate way of helping the poor: give them a job, providing the education and training so they won't need charity. As business people, that's what we do. And if done intentionally, so that our business model is not just about making a profit, lives can be affected in marvelous ways.

> **Early believers didn't pay somebody else to "minister" to the poor. We're *all* called to be ministers.**

If you've been in business for any length of time, you've been told, pressured, or guilted into supporting numerous causes with your hard-earned cash. Most religions teach us to be generous and to give to the poor. In modern times, Christians have been taught to give 10 percent to support, ironically, the "church," meaning their local congregation, which has a paid staff. I say "ironically" because in the New Testament, we are hard pressed to find support for a professional, paid class of ministers that we have today. Yes, there is mention of some folks having their needs provided for so that can devote more time to service projects and other responsibilities. But even the apostle Paul worked his trade as a tentmaker, providing for his own needs, so as to not be a burden to others.

When early believers were asked to give to the poor, the intent was the money would go directly to the poor, and not have someone take a cut off the top. Then, as now, there was to be a personal connection to those we're helping, and not have somebody else to "minister" to the poor for us. If you've gleaned nothing else from my ramblings, hopefully you've come to recognize we're *all* called to be ministers.

That said, I'm not proposing we deny financial help to the needy and to those organizations that help them in our communities. On the contrary, as followers of Jesus, we should be the most generous people on the planet, as we fully recognize everything we have (and are) is a result of God's blessings and gifts. Our response to God's generosity should prompt us to be generous to others.

I can't take credit that my parents started this business. I can't even take credit for them being my parents. I could have been born anywhere in the world into extreme poverty. But since I was born in Wisconsin to hard-working parents, I've had access to a quality education and numerous opportunities. The fact that I'm healthy has more to do with wise health care providers, genetics, and many circumstances beyond my control, such as what my parents fed me, and what I wasn't exposed to in terms of harmful chemicals and pollution than it does with my efforts to make wise choices about my health.

Why haven't I had a rare disease, been severely injured in a car accident, or been consumed by my addictions? I can't explain or justify any of it. All I know is I've been tremendously blessed, and

I feel compelled to help others. But as a business person, "helping others" is too often translated to mean "writing a check" to a nonprofit organization (and getting the business's picture in the paper for doing so). Is this all there is to it? At the risk, once again, of offending those of us with good intentions, philanthropy (loving humankind) should not be a business, but it should be an integral *part* of our businesses.

> **Philanthropy (loving humankind) should not be a business, but it should be an integral part of our businesses.**

When this finally sank in, a whole new world opened up to how much impact we can have through our business. After seeing that the highest level of charity's golden ladder is essentially providing a job, we started thinking how we can use the money we often give to a nonprofit organization to help give people job opportunities and training.

We ended up creating a paid summer intern program for high school students, providing them an opportunity to be in a manufacturing environment with our wonderful staff, who are tremendous mentors. Our scholarship program expanded as we realized many of these students needed financial assistance and guidance in their career choices. And rather than just give money to our local food pantry, we're now funding salaries for them to hire a mentally challenged young man and a struggling single mom.

Most of our decisions about whether to financially support a nonprofit organization are based on how they help train, educate, and provide career opportunities for others. We're no longer fostering dependence on free stuff, but rather giving a measure of dignity and self-respect, as we help individuals be successful.

In all workplaces, as we rub shoulders with our coworkers, we become aware of their needs and struggles, as well as others in our community. Ministering may be as simple as lending a listening ear, providing a meal when someone is injured or ill, helping someone move, or share clothes and resources as able.

There is a trend in businesses for staff to be given "volunteer" time to help in a food pantry, homeless shelter, or mentor in school during working hours. Yes, it is good advertising and PR for the business, but it also engages staff one-on-one with the needs in the community, which fosters compassion and a spirit of gratitude.

There is kingdom work available for us all in more ways than we can imagine.

Goodness in Action

For many of us, the kingdom of God is already in our midst, but, like George Bailey in *It's a Wonderful Life*, we don't even realize it. As His goodness-in-action takes root in our lives and our businesses, like the little mustard seed Jesus talked about, it slowly but surely grows and grows . . . and grows, until we wake up and marvel at all that God has done, is doing, and has yet to do.

I'd like to close by sharing an example of how I believe God's kingdom has come to Edgerton Gear in the form of how our business culture has been and continues to be transformed by the simple concept of helping kids get a start in life.

As mentioned earlier, we have partnered with our local high school to help students find their way in life. The course is called Craftsman with Character. The curriculum is heavy on job shadowing, by allowing students to spend four-fifths (four out of five days a week) of the class time job shadowing machinists, mechanics, and other tradespeople.

The students not only get exposure to what jobs exist, but also gain insight into what makes these skilled tradespeople successful. The fifth day of class is spent in our atrium at Edgerton Gear, which we built to do double duty as a classroom. We discuss with the students what they learned that week job shadowing, as well as delving into topics of character and soft skills that are needed to be employable and successful.

I intended the class to be for whom I call "the lost kids of shop class." These are the kids who are often not deemed "college material," as they often don't excel in a traditional classroom setting. But put them in a shop class, like woodworking, auto mechanics, or welding and machining, and a degree of creative intelligence emerges that is often staggering.

The schools don't often know what to do with this "practical intelligence," so the students spend most of their time in shop classes, which are usually down at the end of a long hall, somewhere in the school building, away from the so-called *real* classrooms.

I was one of those lost kids, not having a clue what I wanted to do when I grew up, but also not fitting into the traditional classroom setting. My family didn't value a college education and, as with many shop kids, my teachers didn't think I had college potential either. It was probably assumed I'd work in a factory or on a farm, where a university degree would be a waste of time and effort.

It was subtly communicated to me that I wasn't as smart as the other kids and therefore didn't have much of a purpose in life. It took many, many years for me to discover that I *do* have worth and talents, and that manufacturing and the trades are not only wonderful career paths, but civilization would not exist without them. So our Craftsman with Character course offers a place for these lost shop kids, to help them find their place in the world.

These kids have taught me more than I can ever write in a book, but one lesson I've learned from them that stands out is the power of righteousness. Although I've heard and read that word many times, I never gave it much thought until this class. It's like oxygen or sunlight; we don't talk about them much; we take them for granted—they will always be there—yet we would shrivel up and die without them. We all subconsciously yearn for righteousness, but we don't consciously recognize it until it's gone.

In fact, we quickly recognize its absence and cry foul, and will even throw temper tantrums and hold rallies and demonstrations to demand it. Yet the world is in desperately short supply of it. Perhaps no one suffers more without it than children, and yet they're the quickest to identify it as missing.

Righteousness. Empires and families collapse without it, surviving and thriving with it. So, when Jesus repeatedly stresses its importance and tells us to seek God's kingdom and His righteousness, I begin to understand—thanks to the Lost Shop Kids.

LOST SHOP KIDS AND GREEK PHILOSOPHY

With the Lost Shop Kids, we do an exercise to help the students think of what character qualities they need in order to be employable. Hypothetically (or maybe not), planet earth is in crisis and needs to colonize a distant planet or moon. Unlike most sci-fi movies, where little or nothing is ever mentioned of welders, electricians, metal fabricators, plumbers, machinists, and other trades, this mission recognizes that tradespeople are the first to go to build the colony. The students are responsible for choosing who joins the mission based on criteria of *truly good*, or virtuous, character qualities.

So the students' job is to make a list of these good character qualities that are necessary for success. Without fail, every class and student, no matter their socioeconomic, cultural, and family backgrounds, comes up with almost the exact same list.

Students who are incredibly poor, from broken homes, where they may be raising themselves (or by a sibling), and/or have suffered from various abuses and are shut down and hardly able to cope with life, nonetheless come up with the same character qualities that are needed to function. A partial list includes *honest, humble, creative, disciplined, responsible, dependable, integrity, teachable, cooperative,* and *respectable*.

These are the same character qualities recognized by most world religions, transcending time and culture. These Lost Shop Kids intuitively have a sense of God's righteousness, true inner goodness, or at least that it's necessary.

As in novels and movies, there are good characters and bad characters; so it is with character development. I've heard numerous times that one of the definitions of *character* is who you are when no one is looking. I don't think this goes far enough in helping us understand what character qualities are necessary in helping students become successful tradespeople.

David Gill, in *Becoming Good*, argues that *virtue* is a better word to describe those attributes that are necessary for good character. He defines virtue as "powers and capabilities . . . that [enable] us to achieve excellently our intended purposes, [in other words] virtues are the *skills* needed to accomplish the task of life."[1]

Gill goes on to discuss Plato's four cardinal virtues of justice, wisdom, courage, and self-control. He notes, "Thomas Aquinas viewed the four cardinal virtues as 'natural' virtues that help us achieve our natural end."[2]

1. Justice: everything is in its proper place, in harmony, fulfilling its purpose
2. Wisdom: making good practical judgments
3. Courage: "readiness to fall in battle"
4. Self-Control: doing what is right despite our appetites

Aristotle, Plato's student, added the fifth virtue of friendship: a relationship of reciprocated goodwill.

It doesn't take much thought to see how these five virtues are needed for everyday life, especially for the craftsman and in the workplace. These virtues of true inner goodness have practical applications in every phase of life. As I spend time with these students, it saddens me to see how emotionally and spiritually beat up some of them are at such a young age. Many of us were no different.

Struggling to be young adults, these kids have been given numerous messages from the media, their peers, families, and society in general that they don't measure up, aren't good enough, talented enough, attractive enough, smart enough, or worthy of anyone's time or attention. Life has often been unfair and unkind. Their own appetites and lusts for more have contributed to their condition, because they have too easily bought into the lies.

Defeated and often despairing, they're cynical that there is any such thing as true goodness, and yet they long for it. Don't we all?

It's exactly this dim hope, this spark of yearning that drew people to Jesus. As with God's kingdom, He not only spoke about true inner goodness, but embodied it and modeled it. So, when He tells us to seek God's kingdom and His true inner goodness, Jesus is calling us out to live in stark contrast to how the world has often treated us.

THE CRAFTSMAN'S CODE

Many of us older machinists see ourselves in the Lost Shop Kids, struggling to know where they fit in and if they have any sense of purpose for being on this earth. Since most of us learn by doing rather than by sitting in a classroom, we have structured the course so the students are actually sitting down in a class only one day a week. The other four days they're out in the shop, job shadowing the older machinists, whom we call the mentors, to not only see firsthand how they do their job but to also catch a glimpse of how important virtuous character qualities are in order to be successful in life.

The true magic of the course happens with these mentors. During the sixteen weeks of the course, the students begin to relationally connect with the mentors, who take an interest in the students, sometimes even helping them outside of work hours.

The students are required to write in a journal every day about what they learned. Since some of them do not have good writing skills, it can be challenging for them to even to write a sentence, so often their entries are very short and simple, such as "Today I learned what a mill is" or "I learned about different kinds of steel."

For the first month or so, their answers are most often about the machining processes involved in making a gear. However, without fail, somewhere around week six or seven, their journal entries start to change. They begin writing things like, "Today I learned Wayne was a drill sergeant in the military" or "Did you know Paul can fix almost anything?" The answers become more about the mentors than machining.

I often like to tell the story of a young man we'll call Josiah. When the school introduced us to Josiah, it warned us that he was one of the most shut down and disengaged students they ever had. The counselors ran out of tools to help this young man. We immediately knew he'd be a challenge, as he wore a hoodie pulled over his head at all times, with his long hair combed over his face, all the way to his chin, like a mask.

During class, he'd put his forehead on the table, never looking up. He obviously didn't want to be at our shop or anywhere associated with school. As he job-shadowed the mentors, he'd barely acknowledge their presence. You could argue that he was being rude, but he was so insecure that we all recognized he felt worthless. He was being raised by a sister and had little, if any, consistent parental figure in his life.

It would be great if I could give you a happy ending of how Josiah's life was miraculously changed and how he went on to have a successful and prosperous life. But that would be a lie. Actually, it might not be a lie, because Josiah's story is still being written, and we've since lost track of him. However, in the five months Josiah was in our lives, we did see such dramatic changes in him that some of his teachers didn't physically recognize him.

He no longer pulled his sweatshirt hood over his head. He cut his hair and looked you in the eye when he carried on a very adult conversation with you. He wasn't our only "miracle" either. Over and over, we see these students transformed over the course of a semester, as they come to recognize they have worth and purpose.

One of the tools we use to change their thought patterns about themselves and the world is to have them memorize the six headings of what we call *The Craftsman's Code*. We talk about it every week, and they have to write it down and say it out loud, as this helps to reprogram their brains and combat all the negative messages they've come to believe about themselves. Here is the code in its entirety:

1. **I'm not the center of the universe**.
   The trades stand on the shoulders of those who have come before us, who learned and contributed to the body of knowledge. Great accomplishments and advancements have happened, and will happen, because of a commitment to the collective good of the trade. I'm always respectful and appreciative of the past and present, recognizing I'm part of the great fraternity of practitioners of my trade.

2. **I do not know everything, nor nearly as much as I think I do.**
   I'm always learning. I value and respect those who teach me. This includes even those who are learning for the first time, as they, too, can teach me new things. No one person can know everything, but collectively, our trade continues to grow in knowledge and skill.

3. There is dignity and purpose in knowing my trade.
There is nothing better in work than to engage my hands, head, and heart. My head learns knowledge, but my hands test if it's true. My hands do the work, but my heart gives it meaning. My heart has passion, but my hands and head give it expression.

4. The world needs me.
The world as we know it would not function without my trade. From basic necessities to extravagant luxuries, my trade supports them all. Therefore, I'll commit to giving my best efforts.

5. Pay is a reward for my efforts, but not my main motivation.
I need money to live, but I do not live for the money. I do not believe in the lie that money will make me happy. Rather, my reward is in the journey—in making something of quality, that is right and that benefits the world, something that uses my creative talents.

6. Every person has unique gifts and talents.
There is only one me. Although I'm always learning, I bring a unique skill set and perspective to every job. It's my responsibility to discover my talents and to apply them in meaningful work.

Now, as a parent, it gives me tremendous joy to hear a teenager say, "I'm not the center of the universe." I then become downright giddy when I hear them recite #2, "I do not know everything, nor nearly as much as I think I do."

Humor aside, we relentlessly pound all six of the above statements into our students. We're able to do this because of the quality of the relationships the mentors build with these students over the four months. By far our greatest satisfaction is when our students graduate from our course, deeply believing in their gut all six of the statements, but especially #4, "The world needs me."

When one or all of our students begin to believe they're not worthless, stupid, and unskilled, but valuable, gifted, and needed, we know the kingdom of God is in our midst.

Remember earlier how I once believed I was destined to be a pastor in a church? Over the years, I've wondered how I could help young people, even thinking we could start a boys ranch or at least be foster parents. I never considered or imagined how our gear shop could impact so many young people. I also never considered how our machinists could be so influential in their lives, shaping and directing these young people's futures. We've become a mentoring culture, not only serving the world through our precision gears, but also through the sharing of our lives. The kingdom of God does that. It takes the mundane, ordinary, and often ignored or disregarded things of life, like blue-collar machinists and the act of making a gear, and turns the whole endeavor and everyone involved into a holy, sacred, and mysterious force that confounds the wisdom of this world.

GOODNESS IN ACTION

The question is: If you've made it this far with me, what does all this look like in your life, in your business? How are you impacting the world? Remember when Jesus was asked when the kingdom of God would come?

He replied, "The coming of the kingdom of God is not something that can be observed, nor will people say, 'Here it is,' or 'There it is,' because the kingdom of God is in your midst." (Luke 17:20–21)

Is the kingdom of God in your midst? It will obviously look different in your business than it does in mine, but there should be some common characteristics that hint we're on the right track in how we approach people, places, and processes.

In terms of *people*: How are you making lives better by providing meaningful employment? What impact are you and your staff making on the lives of those who work for your suppliers and customers? How are you serving them, making their day better by keeping your word, responding in a timely manner, and providing a quality product at a fair price? Do you serve them with joy, peace, humility, and grace, even when they lash out because of stress and pressure in their own lives or businesses?

In terms of *places*: How is your community a better place because you exist? How are your products making the world better, helping it to flourish, to survive and thrive? How is your business contributing to the overall well-being of your community by providing meaningful employment, as well as being a positive role model and good citizen by supporting crucial elements of education, the arts, the environment, sanitation, and local government?

In terms of *processes*: How are you helping the world run more smoothly? How are your products and/or services contributing to infrastructure, food production, information transfer, or any number of products or services that contribute to civilization? Is your business helping transportation, manufacturing, sanitation, or other systems that need to function at a high level for our civilization to exist as we know it?

These are questions we need to ask with some deliberate reflection, for seeking God's kingdom and His goodness takes many forms and has an infinite number of real world applications.

The kingdom of God should be evident in our *people*, *places*, and *processes*.

Over the years, there have been more moments than I can count when being a machinist and business owner was the absolute last thing I wanted in life. But as I said earlier, my father taught me a trade, although I didn't seem to have a choice in the matter. He had me down at the shop before I had even started kindergarten. In the homes of millions of farmers and tradesman over the centuries, children helped as soon as they were able. My mother tells me my grandparents had nine children so they would have more laborers on the farm. This is what life was and still is for many family businesses.

However, for the children, there is often the desire to leave the family farm or shop and strike out and see the world, to see what's out there, to forge their own path, and so on. Sometimes we never come back to our roots but, more often than not, I think we discover home wasn't such a bad place after all, and we appreciate the family business.

Yet for me, even after four decades of working in our gear shop, there are times I abhor it and wonder what my life would have been like if Dad hadn't been an entrepreneur and had the courage to start a gear business where none had existed. What else would I have done for a career? Where would my life have taken me?

As I stated in an earlier chapter, I don't know whether there is any character I resonated with as deeply as I have with George Bailey in *It's a Wonderful Life*. I ache with George in his longing to escape the family business. His younger brother and childhood friends all get opportunities to escape the small town of Bedford Falls, but George stays faithful to the family business, sacrificing his dreams to travel and see the world.

As the movie progresses, with the death of each dream, there is also the miracle of simple obedience, of doing the right thing in all those little moments of daily life. Like George, we often aren't able to see the impact of our daily obedience. We can grow despondent and frustrated, wondering whether we're making a difference at all. In George's case, he is given a gift of seeing what his world would have been like without him. An angel rescues him and proceeds to show how George Bailey's town, family, and friends would have been very different without George's obedience to serve and to constantly exhibit true inner goodness time after time. My kids make fun of me because I get choked up every time I watch the movie. I connect with that film, because I desperately want to know that my life matters.

Seeking God's kingdom is like this. It's in the small moments that others, including ourselves, may not notice or understand how important our choices are for the good of those around us. For example, just this morning, one of our young staff told me how the CPR class we offered saved his grandfather's life last night. As his grandpa collapsed, Sam knew what to do and jumped into action until the ambulance showed up.

Choices are like the proverbial concentric waves from a

pebble thrown into a pool of water, impacting others in ways we can't begin to imagine.

As I've struggled over the years to stay engaged and obedient in the family business, now that I'm in my fifties I can look back and see at least some of the impact our gear shop has made, and it often lifts my mood and spirit. Business and life are often hard and discouraging. The journey is full of setbacks and disappointments. Just when you think you're making progress, sickness, betrayal, financial crisis, or some new calamity hits and takes the wind out of your sails. Yet through faith, perseverance, and struggle—through obedience to do the right thing in even the smallest of choices—the kingdom advances through us.

I'm reminded of a passage in C. S. Lewis's fantasy novel *Perelandra*.[3] The lead character, Ransom, has been sent to Perelandra (Venus) for a mission. He doesn't know what his mission is exactly, but he is told his role is more important than he realizes. He discovers Venus is like earth was when Adam and Eve were the only two humans and before the serpent tempted them to eat from the tree God had told them to avoid.

He meets a woman who is innocent, pure, yet naïve in the ways of good and evil. She has never been faced with evil, but lives in harmony with her creator, Maleldil. Yet Satan sends his representative to Venus to corrupt her and allow evil to enter the planet, as it did on earth. Ransom discovers his mission is to stop him.

An epic battle ensues. Ransom is overwhelmed with the thought that the future of the entire planet lies in his ability to defeat Satan's man. Keep in mind, Lewis lived in England through both World Wars, and the question of evil was not a theoretical one. Millions of young soldiers died during his lifetime in the horrors of war.

On Perelandra, Ransom's fight against evil seems to be vain, as the enemy is relentless and vicious. Ransom questions why he has been sent to fight the battle. Why did God (Maleldil) send him, a weak, middle-aged professor? Against overwhelming odds, the fate of Venus completely depends on Ransom.

Ever feel like that with your business, that *everything* depends on you? Like you're being stretched well beyond your limits, and make one wrong move and the world will come crashing down?

I have, many times, and it's in those moments that my faith and relationship with God make all the difference. Like Ransom, I'm reminded not only that will God not give me more than I can handle (which I've questioned!), but that He asks only one thing of me. "[Ransom] flew back to the comforting words as a child flies back to its mother's

> **God calls us to simply do our best, in the infinite, faithful acts of loving obedience, to do what is right in even the most mundane of choices.**

arms—'to do his best'—or rather, to go on doing his best, for he had really been doing it all along."[4]

We're called to do our best. As we seek the kingdom of God and His righteousness, His true inner goodness lives in and through us, and thus the kingdom of God advances.

A stone may change the course of a river. Our acts of obedience, no matter how small, may change the course of our organizations, those we're called to serve through our work, as well as ourselves. In those moments, the future may not seem to hang in the balance, but can we be certain it doesn't?

The Buddhists and Hindus call it *karma*. The universe seems to be wired so that there is a mysterious, spiritual dynamic to the consequences of our choices. For me, as a follower of Jesus, I believe it's deeper than that. God desires to be intimately involved in the details. We're in the midst of a cosmic battle between good and evil, love and hate, hope and despair. Our arsenal and choice of weapons are not in lofty philosophy and pious religion, but in the infinite, faithful acts of loving obedience, to do our best, to do what is right in even the most mundane of choices.

Call it relevant religion or a practical faith. God sees the big picture and knows best how to strategically utilize his forces. He infiltrates every corner of society by stationing us in sometimes the most nondescript and mundane careers and workplaces, like gear making or other trades and professions. His true inner goodness is relentless and enduring. *We're* His salt of the earth, arresting the rot of our world while drawing out flavor and richness in our relationships and endeavors. *We're* His light of the world, exposing the misdeeds of darkness while lighting the way of how He intended life to be lived.

His kingdom advances choice by choice as we conduct our daily business. As we seek God's kingdom and His righteousness through Jesus, God *imparts* His righteousness to us. We then become God's righteousness, His true goodness, in a broken world. *We* become God's Goodness in Action.

Acknowledgments

While writing the original manuscript, I never imagined it would ever get published. I simply wanted to have a record of how I had come to view work, even in a small gear shop, as significant and life-giving. This perspective is a culmination of a lifelong journey as a lump of clay. For even before I was born, there have been circumstances far beyond coincidence, and people I could never orchestrate, that all played a part in shaping, molding, firing, and glazing my view of life, and ultimately, of God.

There were my grandparents who migrated to America from Germany, Bohemia, and other parts of Europe with a work ethic and skills in masonry, metal working, farming, surveying, logging, and whatever job presented itself to make a living.

There were my parents, who had the courage to start a gear business in a little town in Wisconsin. Their work ethic of excellence, fairness, and serving continues to be part of our family and business DNA.

As a young adult, the late Pete and Shirley Hammond invited me to be part of their family. Pete, an early pioneer of the Faith and Work movement, was especially instrumental in shaping my view of God, family, and the relevance of following Jesus of Nazareth in every aspect of everyday life.

Pete introduced me to another potter and molder on my journey, Paul Stevens of Regent College in Vancouver, B.C. Paul was the first to see the original manuscript. Always the professor, he challenged me to do a major rewrite, gave me a passing grade, and encouraged me to publish. Paul continues to be a tremendous friend and mentor, guiding, nudging, and encouraging in more ways than I can count in the past three decades.

Gerry Fosdal played a pivotal role for a season of upheaval and doubt. He modeled faithfulness, humility, and laughter . . . lots of laughter.

In the past ten years, Brad Smith, Gwen Dewey, Larry Peabody, Judi Melton, Yvonne McKenzie, and the family at Bakke Graduate University have provided inspiration and a place to belong. Brad, Judi, and Larry all took the time to read the early versions and offer invaluable suggestions and edits.

The staff at Edgerton Gear have tolerated and supported my crazy ideas and experiments in building a work community that embodies my parents core values of quality, value, and service.

Mark Sweeney, my agent, somehow believed my writing had value. His encouragement and faith gave this book a life. Mark introduced me to Robb Suggs, a gifted editor who tweaked the manuscript to make it more reader friendly.

The staff at Moody Publishers introduced me to the wonderful and strange world of publishing. Their patience of my ignorance and excitement over this work has carried me along in more ways than they realize.

My three sons (Caleb, Nathan, and Jason) along with our daughters-in-law (Brooke and Hilary) have provided grace, forgiveness, joy, and laughter . . . again, lots of laughter.

Last but not least, my wife, Tracy, has never wavered in her belief in me. She has endured too many of my ramblings and unpredictable moods. We've been married for over thirty years, and I don't know how she did it!

Notes

Chapter 1: Called to Do Business

1. A. Cohen, *Ancient Jewish Proverbs* (Folcroft, PA: Folcroft Library Editions, 1980).

2. Jeffrey B. Van Duzer, *Why Business Matters to God (And What Still Needs to Be Fixed)* (Downers Grove, IL: IVP Academic, 2010), 42.

3. R. Paul Stevens, *The Other Six Days: Vocation, Work, and Ministry in Biblical Perspective* (Grand Rapids: Wm. B. Eerdmans, 1999), 182–83.

4. Dallas Willard, *The Divine Conspiracy: Rediscovering Our Hidden Life in God* (San Francisco: HarperSanFrancisco, 1998), 145.

Chapter 2: Can Modern Business Be Righteous?

1. Troy Segal, "Enron Scandal: The Fall of a Wall Street Darling," Investopedia, updated May 29, 2019, https://www.investopedia.com/updates/enron-scandal-summary/#ixzz4fOP50khF.

2. Jenny Che, "Here's How Outrageous the Pay Gap between CEOs and Workers Is," *Huffington Post*, August 27, 2015, http://www.huffingtonpost.com/entry/ceo-worker-pay-gap_us_55ddc3c7e4b0a40aa3acd1c9.

3. Annamarie Mann and Jim Harter, "The Worldwide Employee Engagement Crisis," Gallup, January 7, 2016, http://www.gallup.com/businessjournal/188033/worldwide-employee-engagement-crisis.aspx.

4. *It's a Wonderful Life*, directed by Frank Capra (Culver City and Encino, CA: RKO Radio Pictures, 1946).

5. *The Chronicles of Narnia: The Lion, the Witch and the Wardrobe*, directed by Andrew Adamson (Auckland, NZ; Prague, CR; Shropshire, UK; Buena Vista Pictures, 2005).

6. C. S. Lewis, *The Lion, the Witch and the Wardrobe*, The Chronicles of Narnia (New York: Macmillan, 1950).

7. R. Paul Stevens, *The Other Six Days: Vocation, Work, and Ministry in Biblical Perspective* (Grand Rapids: Wm. B. Eerdmans, 1999), 18.

Chapter 3: The Pursuit of Purpose

1. Van Duzer, *Why Business Matters to God*, 41–42.

2. John Dalla Costa, *Magnificence at Work: Living Faith in Business* (Ottawa, Canada: Novalis, 2005), 11.

3. Van Duzer, *Why Business Matters to God*, 42.

4. Dalla Costa, *Magnificence at Work*, 54.

Chapter 4: Money and Profit

1. *Happy*, directed by Roco Belic (San Jose, CA; Wadi Rum Films, 2011).

2. R. Paul Stevens, *Doing God's Business: Meaning and Motivation for the Market-place* (Grand Rapids: William B. Eerdmans Pub. Co., 2006), 177.

3. Jacques Ellul, *Money & Power* (Downers Grove, IL: InterVarsity Press, 1984), 75.

4. Ibid.

5. Ibid., 76.

6. Alastair Sooke, "Tulip Mania: The Flowers That Cost More Than Houses," *BBC*, May 3, 2016, http://www.bbc.com/culture/story/20160419-tulip-mania-the-flowers-that-cost-more-than-houses.

7. *Wall Street*, directed by Oliver Stone (Burbank, CA; Twentieth Century Fox, American Entertainment Partners L.P., Amercent Films, 1987).

8. Frank J. Hanna, *What Your Money Means (and How to Use It Well)* (New York: Crossroad Pub. Co., 2008), 29.

9. Ibid.

10. Ibid., 36.

11. Ibid., 66.

12. Helen Keller quoted in Hanna, *What Your Money Means*, 66.

Chapter 5: Is the Golden Rule Good for Business?

1. Jack Wellman, "Parable of the Good Samaritan: Meaning, Summary and Commentary," Patheos, April 24, 2014, http://www.patheos.com/blogs/christiancrier/2014/04/21/parable-of-the-good-samaritan-meaning-summary-and-commentary/.

2. *The Karate Kid*, directed by John G. Avildsen (Hollywood, CA; Columbia Pictures Studios, 1984).

Chapter 6: Relational Transactions

1. *I AM*, directed by Tom Shadyac (Universal City, CA; Shady Acres Entertainment, 2011).

Chapter 7: The Three-Legged Stool

1. Some of the material in this chapter is adapted from "Core Values," Edgerton Gear, http://www.edgertongear.com/core-values.html?.

2. *Merriam-Webster*, s.v. "quality," last updated January 3, 2020, https://www.merriam-webster.com/dictionary/quality.

3. *Merriam-Webster*, s.v. "value," last updated December 26, 2019, https://www.merriam-webster.com/dictionary/value.

4. John Wesley quoted in R. Paul Stevens, *Doing God's Business: Meaning and Motivation for the Marketplace* (Grand Rapids: William B. Eerdmans Pub. Co., 2006), 171.

Chapter 8: Burned Out or Fired Up?

1. R. Paul Stevens, *Doing God's Business: Meaning and Motivation for the Marketplace* (Grand Rapids: William B. Eerdmans Pub. Co., 2006), 35.

2. Ibid., 36.

3. Richard R. Broholm, "Toward Claiming and Identifying Our Ministry in the Work Place," in George Peck and John S. Hoffman, *The Laity in Ministry* (Valley Forge, PA: Judson Press, 1984), 150.

Chapter 9: What Makes a Leader?

1. Edwin H. Friedman, *Generation to Generation: Family Process in Church and Synagogue* (New York: Guilford Press, 1985).

2. Edwin H. Friedman, Edward W. Beal, and Margaret W. Treadwell, *A Failure of Nerve: Leadership in the Age of the Quick Fix: An Edited Manuscript* (Bethesda, MD: Edwin Friedman Estate/Trust, 1999).

3. Ibid., 3–4.

4. David W. Gill, *Becoming Good: Building Moral Character* (Downers Grove, IL: InterVarsity Press, 2000), 32.

5. Friedman, A Failure of Nerve, 14.

6. Ibid., 14.

7. James C. Collins, *Good to Great: Why Some Companies Make the Leap and Others Don't* (New York: HarperBusiness, 2001).

8. Ibid., 22.

9. Ibid., 28.

10. Ibid.

11. Ibid., 12.

12. Ibid.

13. Friedman, *A Failure of Nerve*, 21.

Chapter 10: Community and Culture

1. Edgar H. Schein, *Organizational Culture and Leadership*, 4th ed. (San Francisco: Jossey-Bass, 2010), 219.

2. Stevens, *The Other Six Days: Vocation, Work, and Ministry in Biblical Perspective*, 165–66.

3. Ibid., 189.

4. Matthew B. Crawford, *Shop Class as Soulcraft: An Inquiry into the Value of Work* (New York: Penguin Press, 2009), 40.

5. Ibid., 41–42.

Chapter 11: Betrayal and Failure

1. *Online Etymology Dictionary*, s.v. "sin," http://www.etymonline.com/word/sin.

2. Henry Ford, *American Magazine*, Beverly Smith interview, October 1934; quoted in "Henry Ford Quotations," The Henry Ford, https://www.thehenryford.org/collections-and-research/digital-resources/popular-topics/henry-ford-quotes/.

Chapter 12: Business as Love

1. *Merriam-Webster*, s.v. "philanthropy," last updated January 8, 2020, https://www.merriam-webster.com/dictionary/philanthropy.

2. *Poverty, Inc.* directed by Michael Matheson Miller (Beverly Hills, CA; Brainstorm Media, 2014), DVD.

3. Moses ben Maimon quoted in William E. Diehl and Judith Ruhe Diehl, *It Ain't Over Till It's Over: A User's Guide to the Second Half of Life* (Minneapolis, MN: Augsburg Books, 2003), 129–30.

Chapter 13: Goodness in Action

1. David W. Gill, *Becoming Good: Building Moral Character* (Downers Grove, IL: InterVarsity Press, 2000), 31.

2. Ibid., 97.

3. C. S. Lewis, *Perelandra* (1943; New York: Scribner Classics, 1996).

4. Ibid., 142–43.